HEAD OVER HEELS

by Gail Young

SAMUEL FRENCH

Copyright © 2024 by Gail Young
All Rights Reserved

HEAD OVER HEELS is fully protected under the copyright laws of the British Commonwealth, including Canada, the United States of America, and all other countries of the Copyright Union. All rights, including professional and amateur stage productions, recitation, lecturing, public reading, motion picture, radio broadcasting, television, online/digital production, and the rights of translation into foreign languages are strictly reserved.

ISBN 978-0-573-00068-3

concordtheatricals.co.uk
concordtheatricals.com

FOR PRODUCTION ENQUIRIES

UNITED KINGDOM AND WORLD
EXCLUDING NORTH AMERICA
licensing@concordtheatricals.co.uk
020-7054-7298

NORTH AMERICA
info@concordtheatricals.com
1-866-979-0447

Each title is subject to availability from Concord Theatricals, depending upon country of performance.

CAUTION: Professional and amateur producers are hereby warned that *HEAD OVER HEELS* is subject to a licensing fee. The purchase, renting, lending or use of this book does not constitute a licence to perform this title(s), which licence must be obtained from the appropriate agent prior to any performance. Performance of this title(s) without a licence is a violation of copyright law and may subject the producer and/or presenter of such performances to penalties. Both amateurs and professionals considering a production are strongly advised to apply to the appropriate agent before starting rehearsals, advertising, or booking a theatre. A licensing fee must be paid whether the title is presented for charity or gain and whether or not admission is charged.

This work is published by Samuel French, an imprint of Concord Theatricals Ltd.

The Professional Rights in this play are controlled by Concord Theatricals Ltd.

No one shall make any changes in this title for the purpose of production. No part of this book may be reproduced, stored in a retrieval system, scanned, uploaded, or transmitted in any form, by any means, now known or yet to be invented, including mechanical, electronic, digital, photocopying, recording, videotaping, or otherwise, without the prior written permission of the publisher. No one shall share this title, or part of this title, to any social media or file hosting websites.

The moral right of Gail Young to be identified as author of this work has been asserted in accordance with Section 77 of the Copyright, Designs and Patents Act 1988.

USE OF COPYRIGHTED MUSIC

A licence issued by Concord Theatricals to perform this play does not include permission to use the incidental music specified in this publication. In the United Kingdom: Where the place of performance is already licensed by the PERFORMING RIGHT SOCIETY (PRS) a return of the music used must be made to them. If the place of performance is not so licensed then application should be made to PRS for Music (www.prsformusic.com). A separate and additional licence from PHONOGRAPHIC PERFORMANCE LTD (www.ppluk.com) may be needed whenever commercial recordings are used. Outside the United Kingdom: Please contact the appropriate music licensing authority in your territory for the rights to any incidental music.

USE OF COPYRIGHTED THIRD-PARTY MATERIALS

Licensees are solely responsible for obtaining formal written permission from copyright owners to use copyrighted third-party materials (e.g., artworks, logos) in the performance of this play and are strongly cautioned to do so. If no such permission is obtained by the licensee, then the licensee must use only original materials that the licensee owns and controls. Licensees are solely responsible and liable for clearances of all third-party copyrighted materials, and shall indemnify the copyright owners of the play(s) and their licensing agent, Concord Theatricals Ltd., against any costs, expenses, losses and liabilities arising from the use of such copyrighted third-party materials by licensees.

IMPORTANT BILLING AND CREDIT REQUIREMENTS

If you have obtained performance rights to this title, please refer to your licensing agreement for important billing and credit requirements.

First performed by Tip Top Productions at the Forum Studio Theatre, Chester in October 2018 and directed by Gail Young. Assistant Director Leighton Williams, set and props by Pippa Grundon, sound by Brian Fray, lighting by Mark Shenton, publicity by Paul Croft. The Stage Manager was Pippa Grundon. The cast was as follows:

JILL	Eileen Reisin
ANDY	Richard Taylor
DANNY	Ally Goodman
SALLY	Jane Nugent
CAROL	Rowena Owen
JUDY	Dawn Adams
TINA	Sarah Dyne
GP/PILOT	Derek Weigh
SOLICITOR	Fern Evans
WAITER/GAME SHOW HOST/ POSTMAN/MEDIATOR	Evan Roberts

CHARACTERS

JILL – Our leading lady and a complex role. Age late fifties–sixty. We see her young and in love with Andy from an early age, wedded by her mid-twenties, a doting mum to her son Danny by her early thirties, looking forward to a happy early retirement with her long term hubby.

ANDY – Like Jill, Andy appears to have been content with his family and lot in life. More sporty than his wife, he discovered a love for mountain walking in his later years. And then it transpires that he has been doing more than walking up and down hills and dales with the walking group, especially the titillating trekker that is Tina. A great role for a leading man, both comedic and (at times) villainous!

DANNY – The play follows Danny from his early years to his twenties as the plot guides the audience through the passage of his mum and dad's so-called happy marriage. We see him as a moody defiant teenager, and then as a confident young man in his twenties back with his parents post-college and getting on with life. The marital breakup rocks Danny's world as he tries to support his vulnerable mum while maintaining a relationship with his adulterous father.

SALLY – Jill's younger sister. Menopausal but refusing to admit it! She is still working for a living. Sally has known Andy since she was fourteen and cannot forgive him for doing the dirty on her sister. Supportive to both Jill and Danny in their hour of need and wanting nothing but the very worst for Andy in light of his 'dirty deeds', she views him as a mister who's betrayed her sister, and Sally is baying for his blood.

CAROL – An old schoolfriend of Jill's. Also retired. Like Sally, Carol cannot believe what Andy has done to Jill, and vigorously joins in with the sweary put-downs and insults that the girls heap on him. Carol was divorced ten years ago, and don't we all know it. But she's been hiding a big guilty secret that now eats her up in light of Jill's impending divorce, and it all comes tumbling out in the end.

JUDY – Another old friend of Jill's. One of her disco dancing pals from way back when, reminiscing about Cleopatra's night club and Roxy Music. A lover of prosecco and a believer that there's no problem that a few more drinks won't solve. She has a great vulgar turn of phrase when putting men down, and the best joke about men and Christmas trees.

MS HYDE – Middle-aged. Jill's chosen solicitor, and her legal attack dog for her impending divorce proceedings. A tough old bird who has seen it all before, she is full of both sage and aggressive advice for her client. A marital property war is looming, and Ms Hyde loves a good battle.

- **TINA** – Aged fifty-ish. An attractive trekker with a roving eye that has landed very firmly on Jill's hubby Andy. This is a role with no lines, but maximum impact. The audience has loads of laughs at Tina's expense and this is a role that demands a real talent for both physical comedy and wonderful facial expressions.
- **GP/DR JEFFRIES** – Jill's local doctor. He provides a sympathetic and understanding ear for Jill. Easily doubles up with the role of the Pilot in a later scene.
- **PILOT** – Drunken airline pilot who features in one of the many comedic fantasy sequences in the play. No lines for this character, but plenty of action! Doubles up with the role of Dr Jeffries.
- **WAITER** – Flamboyant, attentive, and blissfully unaware of his customer's marital dispute. To be played by the same actor playing the postman/the mediator/game show host.
- **GAME SHOW HOST** – Larger than life TV game show host who loves the spotlight and chatting up his audience.
- **POSTMAN** – A walk-on-walk-off role with lots of scope for engaging with Jill center stage as he hands her the divorce papers. No lines.
- **MEDIATOR** – Lots of physical comedy in a choreographed routine where the mediator acts as a UN peacekeeper, desperately keeping Andy and Jill apart in a war over ownership of the family home.

SETTING

Minimal set to allow pace needed for quick location changes (e.g.) the pub/home/GP's surgery/solicitors/the car/fantasy sequences etc.

TIME

Set around 2010 in the current day scenes.

Jill and Andy met in the 1970s and wed in the same decade.

AUTHOR'S NOTE

What can I say except that I've been there, and I've got the T-shirt.

Divorce and breaking up are hard for anyone at any time in their lives, but it's a long hard haul to reach retirement with the one you love, and then for it all to fall apart.

I considered therapy to help get to grips with my thoughts, but after a couple of years the lure of the keyboard proved too much, along with the need to laugh in the face of adversity.

So here it is folks.

Head over Heels.

Very loosely based on real events, but very firmly rooted in fantasy too.

It's no exaggeration to say that I had some of the best laughs of my entire life in rehearsals.

My cast were brilliant – so so funny!

The technicians and production team absolutely threw themselves into it.

All of them – amazing – a theatrical arm around my shoulder.

It turned out to be the best therapy I could have ever had.

It worked.

Hope it works for you too.

Gail Young

xx

ABOUT THE AUTHOR

Gail Young has directed and acted with community theatre groups in North West England for many years. Her first full length play *Cheshire Cats* was an Edinburgh Fringe 'Sell Out Show' in 2006 (published by Samuel French, 2011). Since then it has been performed worldwide, translated into other languages, and toured abroad. Her second full length play *Bothered and Bewildered* has also enjoyed similar success after its sell out debut in 2014 (published by Samuel French, 2015). *Bouncing Back* premiered in June 2016 and has also been published by Samuel French. All three plays are comedy dramas with a social conscience, focusing on problems/issues facing women in modern times.

See www.gailyoungplaywright.com for more information about *Head Over Heels*, and email Gail at gailyoungplaywright@gmail.com.

SUGGESTED SONG LIST

Please see the note on the Use of Copyrighted Music on page iii for clearance rights, or footnotes throughout the text for guidance on music use.

ACT ONE

#1 "She Taught Me To Yodel" – Frank Ifield

#2 "Let's Stick Togther" – Roxy Music

#3 "Let's Get It On" by Marvin Gaye

#4 "I Feel Love" by Donna Summer

#5 "Je Taime – Moi Non Plus" by Serge Gainsbourg

#6 "Walk On By" by Burt Bacharach and Hal David

#7 "Memories" by Barbara Streisand

#8 "Climb Ev'ry Mountain" by Irwin Kostal and Margery MacKay

#9 "Only Yesterday" by The Carpenters

#10 "Holiday" by Madonna

#11 "Love Don't Live Here Anymore" by Rose Royce

ACT TWO

#1 "Cars" by Gary Numan

#2 "Little Lies" by Fleetwood Mac

#3 "Band of Gold" by Freda Payne

#4 "Leaving On A Jet Plane" by Peter, Paul and Mary

#5 "Please Mr. Postman" by The Carpenters

#6 "War" by Edwin Starr

#7 "*Hawaii 5 O* Theme" by Morton Stevens

#8 "Life is The Name of the Game" by Bruce Forsyth

#9 "I Will Survive" by Gloria Gaynor

ACT ONE

(Spotlight snaps on **JILL**. *She is sat at a table in a pub with her sister* **SALLY** *and her girlfriends* **JUDY** *and* **CAROL**. **SALLY, JUDY** *and* **CAROL** *are 'frozen' in the moment. The ladies are dressed for a summer day.* **JILL** *is wearing enormous sunglasses.)*

(Suddenly another spot snaps on **ANDY** *[Jill's husband]. He is wearing full mountain walking gear.* **JILL** *passively observes him as he energetically mimes to a '60s yodelling song.* As the song hits the yodelling high-spot he stumbles. The yodel turns into an echoing scream as he falls off the mountain. The spotlight snaps off him.* **JILL** *talks directly to the audience.)*

JILL. I have a hundred fantasies a day like that.

(Lights snap up on **JILL, CAROL, SALLY** *and* **JUDY** *in the pub. Sound effects of pub life.)*

(A **YOUNG MAN** *stands having a drink and chatting on his mobile, but ends up looking aghast at the group of mature women as he overhears the salty language they are using. Aged late fifties/early sixties, all the* **WOMEN** *are well-groomed and dressed for a*

---

* A licence to produce *Head Over Heels* does not include a performance licence for any third-party or copyrighted recordings. Licensees should create their own.

hot summer's day. They are animated and angry.)

SALLY. Fucking wanker!

CAROL. Little shit.

JUDY. Who the bloody hell does he think he is?

SALLY. Geriatric scumbag.

> *(The **YOUNG MAN** holds his hand over the mouthpiece of his phone and leans towards the table.)*

YOUNG MAN. Hey girls, do you think you could keep the language down?

> *(The **WOMEN** speak as one [with the exception of **JILL**].)*

SALLY, CAROL & JUDY. FUCK OFF!

(He backs off and leaves in a hurry.)

SALLY. Bastard!

CAROL. *(Indicating the guy who has just left.)* Him?

SALLY. Not him! Andy! I can't believe it.

JUDY. How long has it been going on Jill?

JILL. Six months…a year…

> *(**JILL** toys with her wedding ring as her voiceover echoes out across the stage.)*

(Voiceover.) I, Jill, take thee Andy to be my lawful wedded husband.

> *(**JILL** is brought back to the present day by **CAROL**'s voice.)*

CAROL. Why didn't you tell us?

JILL. I dunno. I didn't know how to…and then we were meeting up for lunch today…so I thought I'd just come and…

> (**JILL** *can't continue. She fishes for a hanky in her handbag. All the others delve into their bags for a tissue.* **JUDY** *is the first to find one and she hands it to* **JILL**.*)*

JUDY. There you go.

JILL. Thanks.

> (**JILL** *lifts up her sunglasses and dabs the mascara from her eyes. She resembles a very sad panda.*)

Has my mascara run?

SALLY, CAROL & JUDY. NO!

> (**SALLY** *finds a wet wipe in her bag and dabs away at* **JILL**'s *eyes.*)

CAROL. You look absolutely fine.

JUDY. More than fine.

CAROL. You look great.

> (**JILL** *gives them a disbelieving look.*)

SALLY, CAROL & JUDY. You do! You do!

> (**SALLY** *hands* **JILL** *back the sunglasses.* **JILL** *puts them back on.*)

SALLY. I wish I knew how to make it better for you sis.

CAROL. Take it from me – when John left me ten years ago – nothing, NOTHING anyone said made it better!

> (**JUDY** *and* **SALLY** *glare at* **CAROL**.*)*

SALLY. *(Hissing.)* Not now Carol, not now.

JUDY. *(To **JILL**.)* It's always good to talk to friends.

SALLY. Yeah…come on…get it off your chest sis.

*(Pause as they wait for **JILL** to dish the dirt on **ANDY**.)*

JILL. What?

SALLY, CAROL & JUDY. Talk!

*(Spot on **ANDY** in formal evening dress. Lights fade on the pub scene. The other women are frozen in the moment.*

*(**ANDY** shouts over to **JILL**.)*

ANDY. Get a move on will you Jill! We're going to be late.

*(**JILL** jumps up, takes off her sunglasses, picks up her handbag and rushes over to him.)*

JILL. I'm coming. I'm coming.

(She stumbles.)

These bloody shoes!

*(She adjusts her high heels. **ANDY** sighs impatiently.)*

ANDY. I'll go and grab us some good seats.

*(He darts off. **JILL** is left struggling with her shoes. We hear classical musicians warming up.* **JILL** scans the busy room full of concert goers. She spots **ANDY** chatting to **TINA** – an attractive and smartly-dressed woman in her fifties who oozes self confidence. **JILL** tries to attract his attention. **ANDY** ignores her, he's*

---

* A licence to produce *Head Over Heels* does not include a performance licence for any third-party or copyrighted recordings. Licensees should create their own.

deep in an intimate conversation, his and Tina's heads very close together. **JILL** *stands isolated and nervously twists her wedding ring.* **JILL'S VOICEOVER** *is heard over the sound of the waves.)*

JILL'S VOICEOVER. Forsaking all others.

(The sound of the orchestra tuning up swells, turning into the sound of ocean waves as the lights slowly change to green. **TINA** *has her hand on Andy's arm, and casts a sideways glance at* **JILL** *as she casually brushes some lint from the shoulder of Andy's jacket. She whispers in his ear and they both giggle.)*

Welcome to the wonderful world of jealousy! The knot in my stomach grew tighter and tighter because there was just something about that woman...their private joke...the way she kept touching him...the look in her eyes. All my gut instincts made me want to knock ten bells out of her...but good manners stopped me.

*(***TINA*** darts a triumphant knowing look at* **JILL** *and their eyes meet. She turns her attention back to* **ANDY***.)*

I knew right then and there that she knew that I knew what she was doing... I felt it in my bones. And when I thought about what they might be getting up to in private I wanted to rip her dyed-blonde hair out by the roots – in big fat clumps to match her big fat ego.

It was like a tsunami washing over me, sucking me out to sea – and I was helpless...bobbing about in poisonous jealous waves...drowning...

(The sound of the crashing waves fades as **ANDY** *leaves Tina's side and approaches* **JILL**. *Lights return to normal.)*

JILL. You could have waited for me.

ANDY. I didn't realise the seats were numbered till Tina told me. Sorry about that.

JILL. Tina?

ANDY. *(Indicating* **TINA**.*)* Tina from the walking group.

> (**JILL** *looks over towards* **TINA** *who is finishing her drink and looking at the programme.)*

JILL. That's Tina?

ANDY. Yeah.

JILL. From your walking group?

ANDY. Yeah. Shall we go in?

> (**TINA** *glides by them to exit the room. She gives* **JILL** *a little smirk as Beethoven's 5th Symphony, The Victory*, *blasts out.* **ANDY** *scurries off after her as* **JILL** *helplessly watches him go. She turns to the audience...)*

JILL. And in the car on the way home...

> (**ANDY** *re-enters with a huge steering wheel. They both stand in a spotlight as though seated alongside each other in the family car. We hear the car driving along.)*

ANDY. Not a bad venue was it?

JILL. No...not bad.

ANDY. A lot of people there.

JILL. Yeah.

ANDY. And it's always good to support local events isn't it?

---

* A licence to produce *Head Over Heels* does not include a performance licence for any third-party or copyrighted recordings. Licensees should create their own.

JILL. Yeah... I'm just a bit surprised that...

ANDY. What?

JILL. Classical music...

ANDY. What about it?

JILL. We wouldn't normally go to a classical music concert...

ANDY. *(Interrupting.)* I listen to Radio 3 a lot in the car. You'd be amazed.

JILL. You're right. You've never...

ANDY. *(Interrupting.)* It was great wasn't it? Lovely recital.

JILL. Oh yeah...great.

ANDY. Tina is a real fan of classical music.

JILL. Hmmmm.

ANDY. That's why she told me about it. She thought that I... I mean we...we might like to come along and...

JILL. *(Interrupting.)* Yeah...about Tina...

ANDY. She's always organising social events for the group.

JILL. I bet she is.

(Pause as they turn a bend.)

Why does she think you like classical music?

ANDY. We often listen to it when we car share.

JILL. Car share? I thought there was a coach at the club meeting point.

ANDY. On Sundays there's a coach. I'm talking about Wednesdays. When we're driving out to the mid-week walk...you know...

JILL. You and her? I thought John and Steve went with you on Wednesdays?

ANDY. Yes...but the four of us go now...usually...

JILL. Usually?

ANDY. Usually...yeah...

JILL. But sometimes?

*(Pause. **ANDY**'s dropped himself in it.)*

ANDY. Well...sometimes...sometimes it's just me and...er... *(Quietly.)* Tina.

JILL. Who? Just you and who?

(Pause.)

ANDY. Tina...sometimes.

JILL. Just the two of you? Sometimes? You never mentioned that before.

ANDY. I don't know what you're...

JILL. *(Interrupting.)* Out all day in the middle of nowhere? Just the two of you?

ANDY. When you put it like that...

JILL. *(Interrupting.)* So when you strip off butt naked back at the car after the walk and towel yourself down to get changed coz you sweat so much... Tina is stood there...when there's just the two of you?

ANDY. Well...not right next to me.

JILL. Where the bloody hell is she stood then?

ANDY. I er...she er... She doesn't look!

JILL. Really? She doesn't look? SHE DOESN'T LOOK? HOW DO YOU KNOW SHE DOESN'T BLOODY WELL LOOK?

ANDY. You're being ridiculous.

JILL. Am I?

ANDY. We're just good friends.

JILL. Just good friends? Really?

ANDY. You've got male friends. What about Derek at the yoga?

JILL. Yeah – Derek at the yoga! Fully clothed and in a room full of other people. Not naked and sweaty in the middle of nowhere!

ANDY. She's just a good friend that's all.

JILL. Well I think that she wants to be more than good friends – a lot bloody more.

ANDY. I'm not listening to this.

> (**ANDY** *leans across her to switch on the radio. Classical music blares out.** **JILL** *glares at him, and jumps out of the car to rejoin the pub scene. The classical music fades as* **ANDY** *zooms off in the car.)*
>
> (**SALLY, CAROL** *and* **JUDY** *are seated as before. They look at* **JILL**.*)*

CAROL. Classical music?

JILL. Yeah.

SALLY. What the hell is that all about?

CAROL. Since when did Andy like classical music?

JILL. She likes it apparently.

JUDY. 'Tina'?

JILL. Yes.

---

* A licence to produce *Head Over Heels* does not include a performance licence for any third-party or copyrighted recordings. Licensees should create their own.

SALLY. Christ Almighty. He's changed his tune – and I've known him since I was fourteen – since you fell for him and brought him home to our house.

CAROL. My birthday – in town after that Roxy Music gig. Remember? That's when you met him. In that club. What was it called?

JUDY. *(Reminiscing.)* Oh God – yeah – *Cleopatra's*. Those were the days!

CAROL. Besotted you were. The pair of you. Music mad and head over heels in love.

JUDY. How many LPs have you got now Jill? That vinyl stash of yours from the seventies must be worth a bloody fortune by now.

CAROL. The seventies…aah…our era. Those were the days…

SALLY. You were fanatical about your record collection. And there's not a classical note amongst it!

> *(The women freeze in the moment again as a '70s rock song* suddenly blasts out. Lights fade on the pub as **JILL** takes centre stage and dances along to the music. She is nineteen again and in Cleopatra's nightclub.)*
>
> *(**ANDY** enters, He is a 1970s fashion plate – desperately trying to look like Bryan Ferry but just missing the mark. He swaggers over to **JILL**.)*

ANDY. Alright?

JILL. Alright.

ANDY. You dancing?

---

* A licence to produce *Head Over Heels* does not include a performance licence for any third-party or copyrighted recordings. Licensees should create their own.

JILL. You asking?

ANDY. I'm asking.

JILL. I'm dancing.

> *(They dance, desperate to impress the other. Then a slow '70s soul record plays.* They give the audience a knowing look, then smooch. The music ends and bright lights abruptly blind them. They disengage. **ANDY** stands sidestage and combs his hair. **JILL** is centre stage as she addresses the audience.)*

I hate that – when the lights come up at the end. No hiding place then is there? You soon knew if you'd been kissing a frog that night. *(She glances over at **ANDY**.)* Mind you – Andy looked good in the light. Very good in fact.

> *(**ANDY** swaggers over to **JILL**.)*

ANDY. You're not a bad little mover on that dance floor.

JILL. You're not so bad yourself.

ANDY. Can I walk you home?

> *(He offers **JILL** his arm.)*

JILL. Yeah…alright then.

> *(She takes his arm and they very slowly stroll along as she talks to the audience.)*

It's amazing how slow you can walk when you want to and still actually keep moving forward. *(She stops and speaks to **ANDY**.)* This is our house. I won't ask you in coz me Dad can be a bit of an ogre. The third degree and all that.

---

* A licence to produce *Head Over Heels* does not include a performance licence for any third-party or copyrighted recordings. Licensees should create their own.

ANDY. That's alright.

> (**JILL** *goes to leave.*)

No kiss then?

JILL. Cheeky.

ANDY. If you don't ask...

JILL. *(Finishes his sentence with him.)* ...you don't get.

> *(They both laugh.)*

Alright then.

> (**ANDY** *goes to move in. She stops him.*)

But no tongues!

> *(They have a long romantic kiss. He goes to move in again.* **JILL** *holds him back.)*

Gotta go.

> *(He smiles and starts to leave but shouts back.)*

ANDY. What you doing Tuesday night?

JILL. Why?

ANDY. Fancy going to the pictures?

JILL. OK.

ANDY. I'll pick you up at seven.

> (**ANDY** *gives her a cheeky grin and the thumbs up as he exits.* **JILL** *heaves a big romantic sigh and faces the audience. A '70s dance hit plays.*[*] **JILL** *gently sways to the music in a*

---

[*] A licence to produce *Head Over Heels* does not include a performance licence for any third-party or copyrighted recordings. Licensees should create their own.

short choreographed sequence, a lovesick look on her face. Then we hear **SALLY**'s *gentle but insistent voice echoing over the music as the smitten* **JILL** *dances back to the pub.*)

SALLY. *(Voice over.)* Jill... Jill... JILL!

(**JILL** *is now back in the pub scene.*)

Jill? Are you alright?

JILL. I'm OK... I just need another drink.

(**CAROL** *jumps up.*)

CAROL. Don't we all! Here – I'll go to the bar. What are we all having?

JUDY. Prosecco!

SALLY. Me too! Make it a bottle.

(**JUDY** *grabs her bag and hands* **CAROL** *some money.*)

JUDY. Here. Make it two!

(**CAROL** *exits as the others chat to* **JILL**.)

SALLY. Who else knows about his dirty deed?

JILL. No-one...apart from...

SALLY. Danny?

JILL. Yeah.

JUDY. How did he take it?

(**JILL** *gives her companions a bleak look.*)

JILL. Not well... I know he's not a kid anymore...but he can't believe his dad would do that to me...

SALLY. What a bastard! I hope he rots in hell!

JUDY. And her...the bitch!

SALLY. If our dad was still alive he'd go round and give the little shit a good hiding.

JILL. STOP! Both of you...stop it now... Please!

*(**JUDY** and **SALLY** stop ranting. **CAROL** enters with prosecco.)*

CAROL. Come on girls. Let's get this down our necks.

JUDY. There's nothing that a few more glasses of fizz won't solve.

(They all grab a drink. The scene seems to have taken on a festive air as they raise their glasses in a toast.)

SALLY. To Jill.

SALLY, CAROL & JUDY To Jill. Cheers!

*(**SALLY, CAROL** and **JUDY** freeze in the moment. It could almost be a hen night! **JILL** toys with her wedding ring again as we hear her voiceover echoing out.)*

JILL. *(Voiceover.)* To have and to hold from this day forward...

*(**JILL** addresses the audience as the lights dim on the pub scene.)*

Our wedding day was sweet, so sweet *(She closes her eyes and thinks back.)* and if I could just magic it...just magic it back to how it was then...

*(Wedding bells suddenly peal out and **ANDY** rushes on in tails and a top hat carrying a veil and bouquet for **JILL**. She runs over to him, puts on the veil and he gives her the flowers. They stand as though they are at the altar. We hear the vicar's voice.)*

VOICEOVER. You may now kiss the bride.

(They kiss, and walk along to a speeded up "Wedding March". As they do a quick tour of the set waving to the audience as though they are the congregation, they pass the girls in the pub, **CAROL**, **SALLY** and **JUDY** stand and throw a handful of confetti over them and then resume their frozen positions in the pub. **ANDY** picks **JILL** up and carries her over an imaginary threshold. They are both laughing.)*

ANDY. Home sweet home.

(They quickly take off their wedding gear i.e. tails/top hat/veil/bouquet as the wedding bells and music fades out.)

JILL. I love you Andy.

ANDY. And I love you too.

(They kiss.)

You looked so beautiful today Jill…so beautiful.

(He kisses her again and then breaks away – full of the joys of spring.)

God – I'm so happy I could burst! I could you know… I could bloody well burst!

JILL. So could I. *(She looks around.)* And I love our little house.

ANDY. Our own little pad. And it's all ours…well…in twenty-five years it'll be all ours.

---

* A licence to produce *Head Over Heels* does not include a performance licence for any third-party or copyrighted recordings. Licensees should create their own.

JILL. Everyone has a mortgage love.

ANDY. I know. I know. It just seems a long time to be paying for something.

JILL. Hey – look on the bright side. We won't be wasting any money on rent.

ANDY. You're right.

JILL. I know. Shall I put our shiny new kettle on for a cup of tea from our shiny new teapot?

ANDY. Only after we've checked out the shiny new bedrooms! Let's get down and dirty and christen every room in the house.

JILL. All in one night?

ANDY. Well...maybe we'll just start with this room...and the shower...

> *(They end up in a passionate embrace.* **ANDY** *is in the full throes of love and they enthusiastically assume various comical sexual positions while a French love song plays.*)*

JILL. Oh Yes, Yes!!!!!

ANDY. Yess... Yes...!!!!!!

> *(A football whistle suddenly blows and the music abruptly stops.* **JILL** *talks to the audience as* **ANDY** *rushes over to get his sports bag and football boots.)*

JILL. After a while the honeymoon period was over and...

ANDY. Just off out with the lads love. OK?

---

* A licence to produce *Head Over Heels* does not include a performance licence for any third-party or copyrighted recordings. Licensees should create their own.

JILL. Again?

ANDY. Yep. Five-a-side tonight.

JILL. Oh.

ANDY. Won't be back till about eleven – going for a quick pint afterwards.

JILL. Are you still in the Sunday league too?

ANDY. Yeah… You don't mind do you?

> (**JILL** *does mind but thinks better of it.*)

JILL. No… No…course not…that's fine love.

ANDY. I knew you wouldn't mind Doll. Not like Ronny's wife. Christ – the earache she gives him is unbelievable! That marriage is on the rocks – on the rocks! He hasn't spoken to her for over six months – did you know that?

JILL. No…

ANDY. Yeah – he doesn't like to interrupt her! *(Laughs.)* See you later.

> (**ANDY** *gives her a quick peck on the cheek and exits singing "Here We Go Here We Go Here We Go".* **JILL** *watches him leave.* **JUDY**'s *voiceover pulls her back over to the pub scene.*)

JUDY. *(Voiceover.)* Jill… Jill… Jill…

> (**JILL** *ignores* **JUDY** *as she sits down.*)

Jill – are you listening to me? I said he's always been a selfish sod hasn't he?

JILL. No…no…not always…

SALLY. Don't defend the little git.

JILL. He was a good man. Straight as a die…until…until…

CAROL. Until he followed his dick.

JILL. I don't think that...

JUDY. *(Talking over **JILL**.)* That's why men wear ties isn't it? Pointing down...pointing all the way down to their bloody balls!

SALLY. I've never liked him, never! I always felt like he looked down his snotty little nose at me.

JILL. I never knew that.

CAROL. Tuppence ha'penny snob.

SALLY. True!

JILL. When did he...?

SALLY. *(Interrupting.)* He got that from his mother – she never thought our family was good enough.

JILL. But she never...

SALLY. *(Talking over **JILL**.)* What about the first time he had Sunday dinner at our house? He complained that our mum hadn't heated the plates!

JILL. I don't remember...

SALLY. *(Still talking over **JILL**.)* Well I bloody well remember! I wanted to smash the plate over his big fat head.

CAROL. Arrogant...

SALLY. Fucking...

JUDY. Tosser...

> *(The women freeze again in the moment. Spot on **JILL** as she stands and addresses the audience again.)*

JILL. They mean well. The best sister and pals a girl could have. But they're angry and baying for blood – Andy's blood! I haven't got the energy to swear. I haven't slept for a week.

*(Lights up on a GP consulting room. **RECEPTIONIST VOICEOVER** as though we are in a GP's waiting room.)*

RECEPTIONIST VOICEOVER. Mrs Gray for Dr Jeffries. Mrs Gray for Dr Jeffries...

*(**DR JEFFRIES** stands as **JILL** enters.)*

DR JEFFRIES. Mrs Gray?

JILL. Yes.

DR JEFFRIES. Do come on in.

*(**JILL** crosses the stage and takes a seat.)*

Hello.

JILL. Hello Dr Jeffries.

DR JEFFRIES. How are you?

JILL. Fine. I'm fine...

*(Pause as he looks at **JILL** expectantly.)*

DR JEFFRIES. So...why exactly are you here today Mrs Gray?

JILL. I just can't sleep at the moment.

DR JEFFRIES. Oh dear. How long has that been a problem for you?

JILL. About a week.

DR JEFFRIES. Have you any idea why you're not sleeping?

JILL. Yes.

*(Another expectant pause as he waits for more information from **JILL**.)*

DR JEFFRIES. And?

JILL. He's gone...

DR JEFFRIES. Gone?

JILL. Andy...my husband...he's left me...

> (**JILL** *falters – but she holds herself together.*)

DR JEFFRIES. I'm so sorry to hear that Mrs Gray. How long have you been married?

JILL. Thirty-two years.

DR JEFFRIES. Wow... A long time.

JILL. Yes.

DR JEFFRIES. How are you coping?

> (**JILL** *loses control, becoming hysterical. Sleep deprivation is kicking in.*)

JILL. I'm devastated... I don't know what to do with myself. I feel so sick all the time...the divorce diet! That's what they call it isn't it? I just can't eat...and I can't sleep. You'll have to give me something to help me sleep...

DR JEFFRIES. Do you normally sleep well?

> (**JILL** *nods furiously.*)

I'll give you something for the next three nights and that should get you back on course.

JILL. What if it doesn't?

DR JEFFRIES. Come back if it doesn't and we'll talk some more. Do you live on your own?

JILL. My son – Danny – he's still at home.

DR JEFFRIES. Have you got other people you can talk to... confide in?

JILL. Lots...family and friends...you know.

DR JEFFRIES. Good. But if you feel like you need to talk to a counsellor let me know.

> (**JILL** *grabs his hand suddenly, he struggles to free himself.*)

JILL. I just can't sleep! Why can't I sleep?

DR JEFFRIES. Because you're grieving.

> (**JILL** *calms down, surprised by his words.*)

JILL. Grieving?

DR JEFFRIES. Grieving about the end of your marriage. It's natural. You're going through an emotional roller coaster and will be for some time. You will feel down, and you will be angry – but things will eventually settle down. You will sleep again.

> (*He hands* **JILL** *a prescription.*)

Three night's worth of sleeping pills. If you're still struggling to sleep by next week, come back and we'll talk again.

What about eating?

JILL. I feel sick most of the time...

DR JEFFRIES. Your appetite will return Mrs Gray...believe me...very soon.

> (*Lights fade on this scene.* **DR JEFFRIES** *exits.* **JILL** *rejoins the pub scene.*)

CAROL. (*Voiceover.*) Jill... Jill... Jill?

> (**CAROL** *has the pub menu in her hand.*)

What are you eating Jill?

JILL. Mmmmm?

CAROL. What are you eating?

JUDY. I'm starving...

CAROL. Me too. We shouldn't be drinking this much on an empty stomach.

> (**SALLY** *furiously fans herself with the pub menu.*)

SALLY. God I am SO hot! Is it just me or is it really hot today?

JILL, JUDY & CAROL. It's just you.

SALLY. Again?

> (**JILL**, **JUDY** *and* **CAROL** *all nod.* **SALLY** *dabs her forehead with a hanky.*)

These hot flushes are getting me down. Look at me!

JUDY. We've all been there.

CAROL. First sign of the menopause – a broken thermostat.

SALLY. Not me. Not yet. I'm younger than you lot don't forget.

JUDY. Alright Shirley Temple.

CAROL. What are you eating Jill?

JILL. I'm not really that hungry.

JUDY. You'll have to have something.

SALLY. My treat. I know you could do with losing a few pounds but you'll be wasting away at this rate.

> (**JILL** *looks hurt.* **CAROL** *and* **JUDY** *glare at* **SALLY**.)

Sorry... I'm so sorry. That didn't come out right.

JILL. Do you think that's why he left me? Because I'm fat?

SALLY. Nooooo, no...

JUDY. You're not fat!

CAROL. Who said you're fat? Did he say that? Did he?

JILL. No.

JUDY. Did she? The bloody cow.

JILL. No.

JUDY. What did she say then?

JILL. Nothing! I've only met her the once.

SALLY. Bet she's as thin as a rake! Andy's obsessed with people's weight.

JILL. Not always.

SALLY. He is! How much exercise does he do?

CAROL. Football.

JUDY. Cycling.

SALLY. Running.

JILL. Walking...

> *(The women freeze again. A '60s soul record plays.* A spot snaps on **JILL** seated in the pub. Lights on **ANDY** and **TINA** in full walking gear as they stroll arm in arm past **JILL**. They survey their ordinance survey map and peer through binoculars at the mountain scenery. **JILL** passively watches them. Suddenly **TINA** slips. **ANDY** tries to save her. They both fall off the summit, screaming loudly, as they plummet to their deaths.)*

> *(Spot snaps off **ANDY** and **TINA**. Spot stays on **JILL**.)*

---

* A licence to produce *Head Over Heels* does not include a performance licence for any third-party or copyrighted recordings. Licensees should create their own.

(To the audience.) Fantasy one hundred and one.

(Full lights on pub scene and real time resumes.)

CAROL. Yeah...walking. How did he ever end up in that walking group?

JILL. Some people are golf widows. I ended up a 'let's try every sport under the sun until I find something I'm good at' widow.

*(The **WOMEN** murmur sympathy.)*

JUDY. Oh come on everybody. Let's lighten the mood a bit. How do we all fancy eating outside in the beer garden?

SALLY. Only if there's a huge sun umbrella.

CAROL. There's a nice breeze out there. You'll love it Sally.

JUDY. Come on Jill.

JILL. Just give me a minute girls...just give me a minute

*(**CAROL**, **JUDY** and **SALLY** exit with their glasses and bottles of Prosecco, chatting away as they do so. An '80s pop ballad plays* as **JILL** now slips back in time and sets the scene. She ties on her apron, and throws a tablecloth on the pub table which is now part of the kitchen in **JILL**'s house. Flashback continues as **JILL** watches **ANDY** enter. He whistles away and sits at the table. He is dressed casually, has a cigarette in his hand, and reads* The Guardian *newspaper. **JILL** talks to the audience.)*

---

* A licence to produce *Head Over Heels* does not include a performance licence for any third-party or copyrighted recordings. Licensees should create their own.

(Aside.) Bless him. There he is. He used to read *The Guardian* every day. Intellectual? Nah...he only ever read the sports pages! *(To **ANDY**.)* Alright love?

ANDY. *(From behind the paper.)* Yep.

JILL. Fancy a cuppa?

ANDY. *(Still behind the paper.)* Go on then.

JILL. Tea or coffee?

ANDY. Whatever.

JILL. We haven't got any of that in the cupboard.

ANDY. Any of what?

JILL. Whatever.

(Pause.)

So is it tea or coffee that you want?

*(**ANDY** finally looks over the top of his paper.)*

ANDY. Tea...but not too strong. You always make it too strong for me.

*(He goes back behind his paper. **JILL** hurries offstage and immediately returns with mugs of tea.)*

JILL. What's going on in the world today love?

ANDY. What?

JILL. What's the paper got to say today about the state of things?

ANDY. The state of what?

JILL. Things! You know...global warming...the price of fish.

ANDY. The footie season's just kicked off.

(**JILL** *hands him a mug of tea.*)

JILL. There you go. Just how you like it.

(**ANDY** *grunts a 'thank you' from behind the paper.* **JILL** *turns to the audience.*)

(*Aside.*) Then his best mate Tom passed away.

(**ANDY** *drops the newspaper. He is devastated. He puffs away on his fag as* **JILL** *comforts him.*)

Come on now love. Come on.

ANDY. Bloody cancer!

JILL. I know.

ANDY. How many times did I tell him to pack the fags in? How many times did I tell him?

JILL. A million times love. A million times.

ANDY. I said to him – if you want to enjoy your early retirement – if you want it to be a long one – pack the bloody fags in. How many times did I say that to him?

JILL. I know – but it's hard to pack in when someone's sat next to you puffing away like a bloody chimney pot.

ANDY. I know... I know...but I'm packing in the smoking now.

(**JILL** *gives him a disbelieving look.*)

Definitely... I am!

JILL. (*Aside.*) Once Tom died my Andy was a man on a mission. His footballing days might be long gone but there was no way he was going to die. He was going to live forever.

(**ANDY** *jumps up.*)

(*Aside.*) No more fags

(He throws his ciggie on the floor, and stamps on it.)

(Aside.) No more beer.

*(**ANDY** checks out his beer belly – then sucks his stomach in.)*

(Aside.) No more hiding that body away.

*(**ANDY** rips off his shirt and trousers [like a male stripper.] to reveal a tight colorful lycra running strip.)*

(Aside.) And he hit the road – big style

*(He energetically jogs around the stage as **JILL** carries on talking to the audience.)*

He started with little fun runs, you know, just 5k. Well – I say 'just'!

*(**ANDY** doubles over, breathing heavily.)*

(Handing him a bottle of water.) Are you alright love? *(He takes the bottle of water and glugs it down.)* I said are you alright?

*(**ANDY** gives **JILL** the thumbs up – he's too out of breath to speak.)*

Good…good, *(She hands him a huge towel.)* There you go love. Wipe the sweat off you before you get in the car to go home.

*(**ANDY** wipes himself down with the towel as **JILL** chats to the audience.)*

He sweated buckets after a run. Absolute buckets! Niagara Falls had nothing on him. We could have started our own little tourist attraction.

*(**ANDY** stretches his back and straightens up.)*

ANDY. Aaaaaah. That's better. I feel brilliant. Absolutely brilliant!

(He chucks her the towel and the bottle of water and hobbles off. **JILL** *talks to the audience as she puts away the towel and bottle. She places a chair for him to watch the telly when he comes back on set.)*

JILL. And then he'd strip off his sweat-sodden gear and get changed into something nice and dry and warm – all supplied by yours truly. Sometimes I'd drive us back home after the run – you know – while he nodded off in the passenger seat. It was a lazy day after all of his exertions. And this was usually followed by Sunday lunch…followed by…

*(***ANDY*** charges back onto the set as football theme music* blasts out followed by sound effects of a football game in progress.* **ANDY** *sits watching the game and shouting at the telly.* **JILL** *sits flicking through a women's magazine.)*

ANDY. Bloody hell! Come on ref, what are you playing at? Offside? Offside???

JILL. *(Aside.)* One of life's great mysteries…

ANDY. Did you see that? Did you see it? Where do they get these people from? Where?

JILL. What people?

ANDY. Referees. Where do they get them from?

JILL. Referee college?

ANDY. Referee what?

---

* A licence to produce *Head Over Heels* does not include a performance licence for any third-party or copyrighted recordings. Licensees should create their own.

JILL. College.

*(**ANDY** stares at her.)*

ANDY. What are you on about?

JILL. About where referees come from.

ANDY. Why?

JILL. Coz you asked me where…

*(**ANDY** reacts to the sudden cheering on the telly – jumping up and shouting.)*

ANDY. Yessss. Yessss. Come on you Blues. Come On!

*(As **ANDY** continues to watch the telly and react to the game **JILL** talks to the audience.)*

JILL. And so it went on… And on… And on…running and football…football and running…running and football… until…

*(**ANDY** is suddenly on the floor clutching his leg.)*

Oh my God love. What's the matter? What is it?

(She helps him to his feet.)

ANDY. My leg. Christ almighty that hurts. It's me tendons…or Achilles…or sciatica…or summat anyway…

*(**ANDY** winces as he examines his calf and is helped off by **JILL**.)*

JILL. Come on. Off you go. Go and have a lie down…

*(**ANDY** limps off. **JILL** chats to the audience.)*

Poor thing! It's awful to be in that much agony isn't it? Mind you – I do think men have got a low pain threshold. They'd never cope with labour pains like women have to. Oh – that reminds me – hang on a minute...

> (**JILL** *has a lightbulb moment and rushes to consult the date on a suddenly spotlit giant wall calendar.*)

Talking about labour...what day of the month is it? Oh My God... I knew it...it's D day...it's Do it Day!

> (*She shouts offstage.*)

ANDY... ANDY...

ANDY. (*Shouting offstage.*) I'm busy!

JILL. COME HERE... QUICK!!

> (**ANDY** *rushes on wearing paint splattered jeans and T-shirt, and carrying a paint roller.*)

ANDY. Do you want that room decorated today or not? I'm busy!

JILL. It's time.

ANDY. Is it?

JILL. (*She points at the wall calendar.*) I've checked.

ANDY. Are you sure?

JILL. I'm sure.

ANDY. Aren't we a bit young for all this? I don't know...

JILL. What do you mean you don't know? We agreed.

ANDY. I know, I know.

JILL. So come on then.

ANDY. I don't know if I can.

JILL. Course you can.

ANDY. I don't know if I can…to order…you know…it's a lot of pressure.

JILL. Pressure? Pressure? Is that what you think about us making love?

ANDY. I just think that we need to relax about it all.

JILL. *(Interrupting.)* Relax! Relax?

ANDY. Yes.

JILL. So if I just relax then I'll be able to get pregnant?

ANDY. Yes.

JILL. Wow! Thanks. I didn't know that! All these years I've been going to the doctors and the hospital for tests and all I needed to do was to listen to you and just relax.

ANDY. Calm down will you.

JILL. It's alright for you. Blokes don't go on and on and on about it. If I have to listen to one more girl at work saying that her kids are such a blessing.

ANDY. Look on the bright side! Trying is the fun part.

JILL. Said no infertile couple – EVER!

ANDY. *(Offended.)* We're not infertile…we're just…unlucky.

JILL. *(Hormonal.)* I'm in the middle of a good rant here so stop interrupting me will you!

(**ANDY** *shrugs – philosophical about it all.*)

ANDY. It'll happen when we least expect it.

JILL. The next bloody person that says that to me is going to get punched! I can hear all the girls at work now *(She mimics her work colleagues.)* …"Just wait till you have kids"…"Have you tried lying with your legs in the air after sex?"…or "It took me six whole months to finally get pregnant – again"… AGAIN!!!!! And I can't manage it once…just once.

*(**JILL** starts to cry. **ANDY** gives her a hug.)*

ANDY. Hey, hey. Come here love. Come here. I know it hurts… I know it does. And you wouldn't believe the number of lads at work who tell me how lucky I am not to have kids yet…and that hurts me too…a lot.

JILL. We're a right pair aren't we?

(She hugs him back.)

ANDY. Listen – if practice makes perfect our kids will be flawless! Flawless!

*(**JILL** giggles. **ANDY** smiles at her.)*

That's better. Right… I'm going up those stairs to change into me fireman's outfit. You get your nurses kit on and meet me in the bedroom!

*(**ANDY** rushes off. **JILL** chats to the audience.)*

JILL. Poor lad. I put him through the reproductive mill for years. We thought it was never going to happen. And then suddenly – 'Bingo'! I was pregnant! A bouncing baby boy – and we were a little family at last. Happy days! Not sure about the nights though. They were knackering.

*(Immediate sounds of a baby loudly crying. **ANDY** enters yawning and wearing a dressing gown and slippers. He has baby **DANNY** in his arms swaddled in a shawl.)*

ANDY. *(To the baby.)* What's up little guy? You're not a happy bunny tonight are you… *(He yawns again.)* I'm losing track of the days…what day is it tomorrow?

JILL. Wednesday. Give me the baby. Come on Danny. Come to mum. You get back up to bed Andy.

ANDY. Thanks love. I've got a big meeting at work tomorrow.

JILL. Go and get some shut eye.

> *(**ANDY** gives the baby a kiss then hands him over to **JILL**.)*

ANDY. *(To the baby.)* Love you little man...

> *(**ANDY** kisses **JILL** and hugs her from behind.)*

Love you too.

> *(**JILL** giggles and shrugs him off as he kisses her neck.)*

Love you too chubby chops...see you later...

> *(**ANDY** exits. **JILL** talks to the baby.)*

JILL. Did you hear that Danny? He called me 'Chubby Chops' – again! Come on then little man – where do you want to eat out tonight – left or right? Right? *(She breastfeeds **DANNY**.)* Ouch...mind how you go love... aah...that's better *(She sits and talks to the audience and rocks **DANNY** back and forth as walks around the stage.)* I loved these times, just me and the baby in the still of the night. And I was lucky – breastfeeding came easy for me. Look at him – all warm and cuddly with his little lips pressed up against me, snuffling away. What more could you ask for eh?

(She finishes breastfeeding.) Scuse me folks! *(Pops the baby off the set and returns buttoning up her top.)*

Mind you. Motherhood did have it's down sides. For instance – breastfeeding was supposed to be a great workout for me stomach muscles. "Better than sit ups at the gym", the midwife said. Lies, all lies!

> *(**JILL** examines her flabby stomach muscles.)*

Goodbye flat tummy... hello stretch marks!

(She lifts her boobs up to a pert position and drops them.)

Goodbye pert tits… hello matronly bosom. But I quite liked my new boobs! So did Andy!

(She giggles as sits down.)

And our little family was comfortable in its own skin if you know what I mean. There was something really beautiful about not having to play the field or impress anyone anymore. We were happy – really really happy. For a long long time.

(She picks up a women's magazine and flicks through it till she finds the article she is looking for.)

Here it is – I've read a lot of stuff in my time about the secret of a happy marriage. 'What makes a couple happy?' You know what I mean. The sort of thing that you read with a smug smile on your face if you're in that happy place, and that you chuck across the room if you're not. Anyway – according to this *(Points at the article in the magazine.)* the secret formula consists of compromise (Name me a woman who doesn't!), choosing your battles carefully, and good communication.

(She ponders the last item.)

Good communication in a marriage? Now that's a biggie!

*(**ANDY** rushes on, dressed in smart casual gear.)*

ANDY. Where are my car keys?

JILL. Your what?

ANDY. Car keys.

JILL. When did you last have them?

ANDY. Well if I knew that I'd have found them wouldn't I?

JILL. Where've you looked?

ANDY. Everywhere.

JILL. You can't have.

ANDY. I have.

JILL. If you'd looked everywhere you'd have found them.

ANDY. You must have moved them.

JILL. I haven't touched them.

ANDY. You must have.

JILL. I haven't.

ANDY. I always leave them on the table in the hall and they're not there.

JILL. Well they're not there because you mustn't have put them there. When did you last have them?

ANDY. Will you stop asking me that! *You've* moved them!

JILL. Will you stop saying that. I haven't touched them. Think back. What were you wearing the last time you had them?

> (**ANDY** *checks his jacket pockets again. He finds the keys and pulls them out.*)

ANDY. How did they get there?

JILL. You must have...

> (*He has already left.* **JILL** *looks exasperated.*)

A small thing right? But small things add up over the years to become a big heap of things. Like that big heap of towels that he leaves on the bathroom floor every morning! How annoying is that! How hard is it to pick them up, fold them neatly and put them on the towel radiator – HOW HARD IS THAT!!! So I called a family conference...you know...to talk things over. 'communicate'! Danny was a teenager by now – so he was included.

> (**DANNY** *enters dressed as a sulky teenager, followed by* **ANDY** *who snatches Danny's mobile off him and turns it off. They both sit.* **JILL** *sits with a wooden spoon in her hand.*)

DANNY. Do I *have* to be here?

JILL. Now, you know that to stop any arguments the rule at family conferences is that the one with the spoon is the one who speaks.

> (**DANNY** *snatches the spoon off* **JILL.**)

DANNY. Do I have to be here?

> (**JILL** *takes the spoon back.*)

JILL. Yes. It's a family conference so we all need to be here.

> (**ANDY** *holds up his hand.* **JILL** *gives him the spoon.*)

ANDY. Your mum's right. We all need to be here.

> (**DANNY** *snatches the spoon again.*)

DANNY. So? I'm here aren't I? What are we all here for?

> (**JILL** *holds up her hand and* **DANNY** *chucks her the spoon.*)

JILL. We're here because there are things that we need to talk about.

> (**DANNY** *holds up his hand.* **JILL** *hands him the spoon.*)

DANNY. Like?

> (**JILL** *holds up her hand and* **DANNY** *hands her the spoon.*)

JILL. Like the fact that I am not prepared to act as an unpaid servant any more.

*(**ANDY** jumps up and snatches the spoon off **JILL**.)*

ANDY. Unpaid servant? What's that supposed to bloody well mean?

JILL. It means...

ANDY. *(Interrupting.)* Ah ah ah! *(He points at the spoon which he still holds.)*

JILL. Sorry *(She snatches the spoon off him.)* Look, I know that I only work three days a week but I'm fed up of having to pick up and clear up after everyone all the time.

*(**ANDY** snatches the spoon back.)*

ANDY. All the time? Like when? When do you have to pick up after me?

(She tries to take the spoon off him, but he hangs on to it.)

I haven't finished yet. We've had this out before. There is no way that I expect you to pick up after me.

*(He hands **JILL** the spoon.)*

JILL. I didn't say that you expected it. But the fact is that I do – towels on the bathroom floor, smelly undies and socks chucked everywhere and not put in the linen basket, and dirty plates and cups just left lying around.

*(**DANNY** goes to snatch the spoon off **JILL** and she raps the back of his hand with it.)*

Wait will you!

DANNY. Shit...that hurt!

> (**ANDY** *grabs the spoon off* **JILL** *and raps* **DANNY** *across the head with it.*)

What the fuck!

ANDY. Pack that swearing in... I've told you before.

> (**JILL** *grabs the spoon off* **ANDY** *and stands and holds it aloft as* **DANNY** *and* **ANDY** *argue about* **DANNY**'s *swearing. They cannot hear* **JILL** *until she shouts over their voices.*)

JILL. I have the spoon... I have the spoon! I HAVE THE SPOON!

> (**ANDY** *and* **DANNY** *burst out laughing.*)

ANDY & DANNY. (*Mocking* **JILL** *in unison.*) I have the spoon! I have the spoon!

ANDY. Alright. Alright 'Mistress of the Spoon'. We'll tidy up in future – but only on condition that you stop being such a martyr about it all. Deal?

> (*They both stare at* **JILL**.)

JILL. Deal.

> (**DANNY** *picks up the spoon.*)

DANNY. Can I go now?

JILL. Meeting over.

> (**DANNY** *drops the spoon, picks up his phone and exits.* **ANDY** *picks the spoon up.*)

ANDY. (*Following* **DANNY** *off and brandishing the spoon at him.*) Make sure you're back home before ten tonight you...you've got school tomorrow remember...

> (**JILL** *talks to the audience.*)

JILL. Relationships live and die not by the sword, but by how well you communicate. And we did communicate – a lot! We never ever stopped talking… or arguing…or laughing…

(She picks up the magazine and reads from it.)

"Choose your battles carefully" *(Thinks.)* Well we bickered a fair bit – like over the towels on the bathroom floor, who does the ironing, and putting the cap back on the toothpaste – but big things? No – we never really battled about big things until…

*(A spotlight suddenly snaps up on **TINA**. She is in full mountain walking regalia with immaculate hair and make-up. She holds a small hand mirror and admires her reflection.)*

(Aside.) All that striding up and down hasn't done her legs any good.

(A musical showtune plays. **TINA** mimes to it as she climbs a mountain. **JILL** watches. **TINA** screams as she stumbles and falls off the summit. The spot snaps off. **JILL** smiles at the audience.)*

One hundred and two!

(Pause.)

Jumping ahead though aren't I?

*(**JILL** looks back at the magazine.)*

Oh yes… 'Choosing your battles carefully' *(Pause.)* Remember his injury? The one that put paid to the football and the running? Well he soon had another

---

* A licence to produce *Head Over Heels* does not include a performance licence for any third-party or copyrighted recordings. Licensees should create their own.

problem. He's at that age isn't he? It's just a shame it wasn't erectile dysfunction!

(**ANDY** *rushes on brandishing a box of pills.*)

ANDY. Arthritis!

JILL. No

ANDY. Yep – that pain in my hip and my thigh. It's not sciatica. It's bloody arthritis!

JILL. No

ANDY. Yes! *(Holds up his medication.)* So that means that I've got to take these. And it won't get better. I might end up with a hip operation in a few years, and you know how much I hate hospitals!

JILL. Don't get all hot and bothered about it. Hip replacements aren't a big deal nowadays.

ANDY. But it means that I won't be able to go mountain walking with... *(He stops himself.)*

JILL. With who?

ANDY. The club. I won't be able to go walking with the club.

(He sits and stares at the medication.)

JILL. Look Andy. There's got to be other ways of dealing with arthritis *(She chats to the audience as he continues to stare at his tablets.)* And like the Florence Nightingale kind of gal that I am I found out about a fab diet to beat arthritis. So I put him on it for six weeks – and at the end...

(**ANDY** *suddenly bounds up from his chair. He is overjoyed.*)

ANDY. It's gone! The pain's gone. *(He hugs* **JILL**.*)* Thanks love. Thanks.

(JILL hugs him back.)

I'd better get my walking gear ready. Sunday today and the rambling group are doing my favourite route in Snowdonia. I don't want to miss it do I?

(He rushes off. JILL turns to the audience.)

JILL. Just write MUG on my forehead will you…please! In indelible ink in big fat letters. 'M.U.G… MUG'! SOMEBODY write it across my forehead! What's those things that get released round your body when you exercise? Endorphins? That's them isn't it…endorphins. Apparently – after exercise – endorphins are released into your body and leave you feeling energised and in a better mood for the rest of the day. But the only problem was that he was feeling like that – energised and in a better mood – when he was going for a drink in the pub afterwards with you know who! *(Pause.)* … But he had a passion for the mountains. A real passion. And that's what makes the world go round isn't it? Passion. So I never begrudged him that feeling for the mountains, never…until…

*(**ANDY** rushes back on in his walking gear and carrying his rucksack.)*

ANDY. Right. All set. See you later.

JILL. What time do you think you'll be back?

ANDY. Not sure. You know what it's like. Got to make the most of the daylight hours while we've still got them. You don't mind do you?

*(He rushes off. **JILL** addresses the audience.)*

JILL. I didn't mind coz we had plenty of other days in the week to do stuff together. Well – I say 'plenty'…

*(**ANDY** rushes on again in his walking gear. It is a Groundhog Day moment.)*

ANDY. Right. All set. See you later

JILL. But it's Wednesday. I thought the club only walked on a Sunday.

ANDY. There's a little group of us doing a mid-week walk now as well, and...

JILL. And what?

ANDY. Well...we've organised a few weekends away. And a week up in Scotland in the Spring. You don't mind do you? Gotta dash.

JILL. Andy... I...

> *(He's already gone. **JILL** stares at the audience.)*
>
> *(**ANDY** re-enters as before. Another Groundhog Day moment.)*

ANDY. Right. All set... I'm just off to...

JILL. *(Interrupting.)* I know where you're going, and I know you're gonna be out all day. I know that!

> *(Momentary pause as **ANDY** looks slightly guilty – but he soon overcomes it.)*

ANDY. Right... All set... See you later!

> *(**ANDY** dashes off again. **JILL** watches him go. Suspicions are now strong. **DANNY** enters in his pyjamas carrying a glass of orange juice. He's now in his early twenties.)*

DANNY. Alright?

JILL. Yeah.

DANNY. Where's Dad?

JILL. Up a mountain somewhere by now.

DANNY. Again? *(Yawns.)* …What time's Sunday lunch Mum?

JILL. Whenever you want. Your Dad doesn't know what time he'll be back.

DANNY. Well don't bother making me any then. I'm off out later. Sam and Mike are picking me up about seven so I'll get something while I'm out.

JILL. OK.

>   (**DANNY** *yawns.*)

DANNY. I'm knackered. I'm off back to bed for a couple of hours.

JILL. I'm not surprised. I think I heard the dawn chorus when you rolled home.

DANNY. Did I wake you up?

JILL. Mums don't sleep till the key is in the latch.

DANNY. Sorry.

JILL. Hey – don't apologise. It's just me! You know what I'm like.

>   *(He turns to leave, but her words make him turn back.)*

So – how's things with you?

>   (**DANNY** *is horrified to be asked about his private life. He's at that age.*)

DANNY. OK.

JILL. Still seeing Alexandra?

DANNY. Nah.

JILL. Why not?

DANNY. Too quiet for me. I mean – she's a nice girl and all that – but just too quiet. Hard work…

JILL. That's a shame. How many girls is that this year then?

DANNY. I'm not keeping count! What is this? The bloody third degree?

JILL. I really liked Alex...

DANNY. Stop nagging will you mum.

JILL. She seemed like such a nice girl...

DANNY. Mum! Pack it in will you!

JILL. Alright, alright... It's just that your Dad and I were...

(**DANNY** *finishes the sentence for his mum. He's heard it all before.*)

DANNY. '...married at your age'. Yes I know Mum. But it's not the seventies now.

JILL. I know, I know...

DANNY. Don't ever start saving for a big hat! I'm never getting married...to anyone.

JILL. No?

DANNY. What's the point? A lot of my mate's parents gave up years ago...got divorced.

JILL. Really?

DANNY. Yeah! Rob's parents have just split up. Did I tell you?

JILL. No.

DANNY. A right old ding dong's going on there about the house and who's gonna have what. Mind you, Rob said he's not surprised. He said they were always bloody rowing.

JILL. Everyone argues. Me and your Dad do.

DANNY. I know – but not like them though. And you always make up in the end.

*(Pause. **JILL** is near to tears. **DANNY** notices.)*

Mum?

*(**JILL** tries to evade his gaze. He follows her.)*

Mum? What's the matter?

JILL. Nothing...nothing.

DANNY. You're not ill are you?

*(**JILL** shakes her head.)*

Is it Dad? Is there something wrong with Dad?

JILL. *(Nodding.)* Mmmmmmm.

DANNY. What? What is it?

*(**JILL** wipes a few tears away.)*

You're scaring me now. It's serious isn't it? Is it Cancer?

JILL. No! ...no...it's not Cancer...

DANNY. Well what is it then? What's up with him?

*(Pause as **JILL** gathers herself together.)*

JILL. *(Quietly.)* I think he's seeing another woman.

DANNY. Sorry? Did you just say he's seeing another woman?

JILL. I think he is...yes...

DANNY. Who?

JILL. Tina...

DANNY. Tina? Who's Tina?

JILL. She's in the same walking group as him.

DANNY. No! No...he'd *never* do that. Never! What makes you think that?

JILL. I've just got this feeling.

DANNY. Mum – you've got to stop thinking like that. Do you hear me? She's probably just a good friend. You know what it's like when sporty types get together. 'Team bonding' and all that horseshit.

JILL. Do you think so?

DANNY. Talk to him about if you're upset about it.

JILL. I've tried.

DANNY. And?

JILL. He said they're just friends.

DANNY. There you go.

JILL. But what if...

DANNY. What if what?

JILL. What if he's lying?

DANNY. Dad? Lying? He couldn't tell a lie to save his life – you know that.

JILL. I used to.

DANNY. Mum! Come on! Give him a bloody break will you!

*(Expectant pause as **DANNY** waits for a reply from his mum.)*

If he says they're just good friends...that's all they are... Dad's one of the good guys remember?

JILL. Is he?

DANNY. Oh – you're just being fucking stupid now... I'm not listening to this!

(He storms out in a huff.)

*(Pause as **JILL** gathers her thoughts. She talks to the audience.)*

JILL. 'Just good friends...just good friends'. That's a classic isn't it? God... I so wanted that to be true and things to go back to how they were...back to yesterday.

(A '70s pop/folk song plays.* She sways gently, trying to comfort herself with past memories. The music fades to a low level.)

So by the time Andy got back from his walk I was guilt ridden...guilt ridden that I'd doubted him.

*(**ANDY** enters and the music fades out.)*

Hiya. Had a good day's walking?

(She helps him off with his backpack.)

Fancy a drink? There's some beer in the fridge.

ANDY. No thanks.

JILL. How about a gin and tonic before you have a shower? I fancy one myself.

*(She goes to make them a drink. **ANDY**'s words stop her in her tracks.)*

ANDY. Jill. I need to talk to you.

JILL. What about?

(Long pause.)

Well – what is it?

(Pause.)

---

* A licence to produce *Head Over Heels* does not include a performance licence for any third-party or copyrighted recordings. Licensees should create their own.

Tell me.

(**ANDY** *mumbles something.*)

I can't hear you.

(**ANDY** *speaks loudly and clearly.*)

ANDY. I think we should split up.

(*Pause.*)

JILL. What did you say?

ANDY. I said… I think we should split up.

(*Long pause.*)

JILL. I thought that was what you said…

(*Long pause.*)

ANDY. I've been thinking it over and the truth is…

JILL. (*Interrupting.*) It's her isn't it?

ANDY. Who?

JILL. Tina. It's her.

ANDY. She's got nothing to do with…

JILL. (*Interrupting.*) It is her… It's Tina isn't it?

ANDY. Look Jill, I don't think that…

JILL. I knew it. I knew it! I was right all along wasn't I? The conniving little bitch.

ANDY. Now that's enough!

JILL. I was bloody right all along and you… YOU …told me I was imagining things…that you were just good friends! Is she the one?

ANDY. Stop it will…

JILL. Admit it. Go on. You're leaving me for her aren't you?

ANDY. No... I...

JILL. You've been carrying on with her all along haven't you? Say it... SAY IT WILL YOU!!

(Pause.)

ANDY. We've formed an attachment.

JILL. You've 'formed an attachment'! What the hell does that mean?

ANDY. It means...

JILL. *(Interrupting.)* Have you slept with her?

ANDY. Jill...look...this isn't getting us anywhere...

JILL. *(Interrupting.)* Have you fucked her?

ANDY. I ...do you have to swear?

JILL. HAVE YOU FUCKED HER!

(Pause.)

ANDY. She didn't want it go any further until I...

JILL. Until you've got shot of me? Is that what she wants? 'No full penetration without representation' Christ almighty – it's Anne Boleyn and Henry the VIII all over again!

ANDY. I have not had sex with...

JILL. *(Interrupting.)* Oh stop it will you. You're starting to sound like Bill Clinton now!

(Long pause.)

Why Andy? Why?

*(Sound of massive ocean waves as **ANDY** starts to tell her why he is leaving. We see him speaking but can't hear him. There is a voiceover from **JILL** over the sound of the*

> *waves. She stands isolated, and* **ANDY** *sits talking/explaining – but we cannot hear him.)*

JILL'S VOICE OVER. And there it was again. The tsunami... those giant waves... I felt like I was drowning and he was standing on the shore while I was being dragged to a place I didn't want to go... tsunamis...eruptions... they rip homes apart don't they? And that's what was happening to me...to my family...we were being ripped apart...and all the time he was talking I could hardly hear what he was saying...and the waves kept coming... and I cried...little salty tears in that huge ocean of betrayal...

> *(The sound of the waves fades away.)*

ANDY. I can't live a lie anymore. I don't love you... I love Tina...and I want a divorce

> *(Pause.)*

Did you hear me?

> *(Long pause.)*

JILL. What now?

ANDY. I'm going to her house tonight. I just need to get some clothes. I'll come back for the rest of my stuff in a couple of days.

> *(His mobile phone rings. He answers it. It's obviously* **TINA**.*)*

Hi...yeah...yeah...it's all come to a head... I'll be round soon...yeah... I just need to pack a few things before...

> *(**JILL** suddenly snatches the mobile off him and shouts down the phone.)*

JILL. You finally got what you fucking wanted didn't you? You got him in the end!

(**ANDY** *snatches the phone back.*)

ANDY. Sorry about that Tina. Yep…see you later. *(He hangs up. Big sigh.)* Did you have to swear?

JILL. Sorry?

ANDY. It's just so…

JILL. So what?

ANDY. So…common…

(**JILL** *is incredulous at his remark.*)

JILL. Well – I might say 'fuck' …but I don't go round fucking other people's husbands!

(**DANNY** *suddenly enters. He is ready to go out and has his earphones on happily listening to music. He has not heard their argument.* **JILL** *and* **ANDY** *stare at him. He finally realises, and takes the earphones out.*)

DANNY. I'm off out in a minute – the lads are picking me up. *(Looks at his mum.)* Are you alright?

(Pause.)

JILL. Your Dad's got something to tell you.

DANNY. *(He looks at* **ANDY**.*)* What's going on?

ANDY. I…er…

(Pause.)

JILL. Tell him Andy?

DANNY. What is it?

(Pause.)

ANDY. I...er...

> (**ANDY** *stares at* **JILL**, *almost pleading with her to tell* **DANNY** *the news.*)

JILL. TELL HIM ANDY!

ANDY. Your mum and I are splitting up.

> (*Pause.*)

JILL. That's not strictly true. Your Dad is leaving me.

DANNY. Leaving you?

JILL. For Tina.

DANNY. Tina?

> (**DANNY** *looks to* **ANDY** *for an answer.*)

JILL. From the walking group.

> (**DANNY** *confronts his Dad.*)

DANNY. Dad? What's going on? ... Dad? ...

> (**DANNY** *waits for an answer.*)

ANDY. I've got to pack some stuff.

> (*He barges past* **DANNY** *and exits.*)

> (*Pause.*)

> (**JILL** *starts to cry.* **DANNY** *comforts her.*)

DANNY. Oh mum...mum...come here...

JILL. I'm sorry love. I'm so sorry.

DANNY. I'll cancel the night out with the lads...stay here with you.

JILL. No! Don't...don't. I don't want you here when your Dad goes...you go on out.

DANNY. No...no.

JILL. Yes. I mean it.

> *(There is the sound of a car horn.)*

There's your lift. Go on – go on – I'll be alright...really... go on.

> *(She pushes him to the door.)*

DANNY. I'll ring you later. Be back early too...

> *(He goes to leave, but rushes back to her and gives her a long silent hug before he quickly exits.)*
>
> *(**ANDY** enters carrying a small suitcase. He picks up his rucksack and car keys.)*

ANDY. Well... I'm off then.

> *(Pause.)*

JILL. Right.

> *(Pause.)*

ANDY. I'll be in touch.

JILL. Yeah.

ANDY. You know...about money...and things.

JILL. Mmmmmm.

ANDY. So...

JILL. Oh for Christ's sake – just bloody well go will you!

> *(**ANDY** exits. **JILL** watches him go and then speaks to the audience.)*

And just like that he was gone…after thirty-two years…like a puff of smoke…puff…like he…like we…never existed…were never a couple…were never 'us'.

> (**JILL** *picks up the magazine and reads aloud.*)

What's next on the list for long lasting relationships? … Oh yeah… "Sometimes when we enter into a long-term relationship, we put ourselves second, behind the other person's needs and desires. Two people rarely have exactly the same wants and desires out of life – that's just a fantasy…" *(She chucks the magazine on the table and stands centre stage.)* Never a truer word said coz that's what it all felt like now. Like one big fantasy!

> (*Sudden loud laughter offstage from* **SALLY**, **CAROL** *and* **JUDY**, *they call out to* **JILL** *in a voiceover. We are back in the present day.*)

SALLY, CAROL & JUDY. Jill… Jill… Jill?

> (*Lights have changed to a large central spot on* **JILL**. **SALLY, CAROL** *and* **JUDY** *enter, quite tipsy and jolly, with a glass of Prosecco for her.*)

SALLY. Where've you been Jill?

CAROL. Come on outside – it's lovely out there in the beer garden.

JUDY. And the food looks fab.

SALLY. We've ordered some of those sharing platters. They'll be here in five minutes.

> (**CAROL** *hands* **JILL** *a glass of Prosecco.*)

CAROL. Come on Jill. Time to down a few more bubbles.

JUDY. Drown your sorrows girl.

(**JILL** *necks the glass of Prosecco in one with the other women chanting 'Down in one. Down in one'. The girls cheer as she knocks it back.*)

SALLY. Getting her mojo back I think!

JILL. Carol – have you got the name of that solicitor you used when you and John split up?

CAROL. Of course. Olivia Hyde.

JUDY. Was she any good?

CAROL. Ruthless.

JUDY. Excellent!

SALLY. What was her advice to you Carol when John walked out?

CAROL. Shut the door and CELEBRATE!

(*The other women cheer and leave the set singing an '80s pop song.** **JILL** *hangs back and the spotlight on her tightens. She looks at her empty glass and speaks to the audience.*)

JILL. Cheers… (*She chokes on the word and starts to softly cry.*)

(*A '70s soul song plays** *as the spotlight on* **JILL** *fades very slowly to blackout.*)

End of Act One
Interval

---

* A licence to produce *Head Over Heels* does not include a performance licence for any third-party or copyrighted recordings. Licensees should create their own.

ACT TWO

(A '70s synth-pop song plays.*)

(Spot fades up on **JILL** *in a daydream, sat with her solicitor* **MS HYDE**. **MS HYDE** *is in semi darkness – 'frozen' in the moment. Another spot fades up on* **ANDY** *and* **TINA** *driving along in an open-topped vehicle, wearing sunglasses,* **TINA**'s *scarf fluttering in the breeze.* **TINA** *snuggles up to* **ANDY**, *he puts his arm around her shoulder and now has one hand on the steering wheel. They steal a kiss and in slow motion, the song morphs into the sound of a car's brakes screeching.* **TINA** *is screaming but we cannot hear her.* **ANDY** *desperately tries to control the steering wheel. They career off stage in slow motion as we hear the sound of an almighty car crash.* **JILL** *addresses the audience.)*

JILL. Fantasy one hundred and three.

(Lights up on the solicitor's office. **JILL** *and* **MS HYDE** *are both sat at the desk. The sign for the office reads 'DITCHEM, QUICK & HYDE. DIVORCE SOLICITORS'.)*

MS HYDE. Mrs Gray? Mrs Gray?

JILL. Sorry?

---

* A licence to produce *Head Over Heels* does not include a performance licence for any third-party or copyrighted recordings. Licensees should create their own.

MS HYDE. I was just saying that from what you've told me you want to file for divorce on the grounds of adultery?

JILL. Yes... I mean no... Oh – I don't know.

MS HYDE. You don't know?

JILL. It all seems a bit soon.

MS HYDE. A bit soon for what?

JILL. Divorce. It's so...final.

MS HYDE. Are you hoping for a reconciliation?

JILL. I'm not sure...not yet... I mean... *(She forces a smile.)*

*(***MS HYDE*** smiles back.)*

MS HYDE. I understand. It's still early days. So there's no need to rush into anything at this point.

JILL. I'm not even sure I've done the right thing coming to see you today...

MS HYDE. I can assure you that you've done *absolutely* the right thing seeing me today! You need to know what your rights are.

JILL. I'm so muddled up about it all – I just don't know where to start.

MS HYDE. Well – you've both taken early retirement which means that a 50/50 split of your joint assets should be relatively straightforward.

JILL. I see.

MS HYDE. And your son is an adult so there are no custody issues which makes things a lot easier for you.

JILL. Danny is so upset about it all.

MS HYDE. I know. It must be hard for you both. Do you know if your husband has seen a solicitor yet?

JILL. No... I haven't seen him since he... *(She falters.)*

MS HYDE. Since he left? *(Consults her notes.)* Four weeks ago?

> *(**JILL** nods her head.)*

It would be useful if you can remain on speaking terms with him. For instance – we really need to know the name and address of his solicitor, and I would advise that you jointly see a mediator. It's much better to reach a joint agreement about splitting your assets rather than taking things to court – less expensive for you both.

JILL. To court? I won't have to go to court will I?

MS HYDE. Highly unlikely.

JILL. God – I'd hate that. Having our dirty linen aired in public.

MS HYDE. It shouldn't come to that. But if it did you'd need to remember that there are three sides to every story in a court of law. Your side, his side, and the full story.

JILL. Are you saying that whoever tells the best story wins?

MS HYDE. Not exactly.

JILL. Does the fact that he's carrying on with another woman mean anything in a financial settlement?

MS HYDE. No. But hopefully he's only morally bankrupt so you'll still get 50% of your joint assets.

> *(They both laugh.)*

JILL. Is it true that the marriage can be dissolved if we live apart for two years?

MS HYDE. Yes – if both parties are agreeable.

JILL. I think I might want to do that… I don't want to rush into anything…or do any name calling.

MS HYDE. Are you sure about that? He hasn't been that considerate about you remember.

JILL. I don't want our son – Danny – to see us writing horrible things about each other in divorce papers.

MS HYDE. That is certainly food for thought. But in my experience a long separation just gives your husband more time to hide his money away. Plus the third party...

JILL. Third party?

MS HYDE. Tina is it? *(Refers to her notes.)* Yes...here she is...the Titillating Trekker that is Tina! From experience I would say that she will definitely be wittering away in your husband's ear or one of his many other orifices as we speak. You can't underestimate her influence in these matters from now on.

(**JILL** *looks stunned.*)

You look shell shocked.

JILL. I am.

MS HYDE. Can I suggest that we leave it there for today. Could you try and arrange meeting up with your husband as soon as possible to discuss the way forward? And agree on a mediator that you can see? I'll email you some names of mediators that you could contact. Is that OK?

JILL. It's all so nerve wracking. Oh God help me – I just want to do the right thing!

MS HYDE. God works wonders now and then Jill – but for this you need a tough old bird like me. I'm sure that between myself and the mediator we'll do our very best for you.

JILL. Thanks Miss Hyde.

MS HYDE. Call me Olivia.

JILL. Thanks... Olivia.

(*They shake hands.* **MS HYDE** *turns back.*)

MS HYDE. Oh – and by the way – I'll write out to you confirming all that we've discussed today plus of course the legal costs that you'll incur going forward. Bye Jill.

(**MS HYDE** *gathers her papers and exits. Lights fade on the scene. Sound of a gavel and then the booming/echoing voiceover of a* **JUDGE***'s voice as a spot snaps up on* **JILL**.)

JUDGE'S VOICEOVER. Do you, Jill Gray, promise to pay your legal bills, all of your legal bills, and nothing but your legal bills till you and Andy do part?

JILL. I do.

(**JILL** *talks directly to the audience.*)

That's me financially stuffed for the next twelve months.

(*Jill's mobile rings. In another spotlight we see* **SALLY** *on her mobile.*)

Hiya Sis.

SALLY. How did it go at the solicitors?

JILL. OK I suppose.

SALLY. I hope you told her everything.

JILL. Yeah yeah... I'm still in shock though.

SALLY. I'm not surprised. The things that bastard has...

JILL. (*Interrupting.*) Not Andy – the legal costs!

SALLY. That bad?

JILL. Make crime pay – become a lawyer!

SALLY. Oh no – that bad eh?

JILL. And we're going to have to see a mediator as well – so I'm not rushing anything. Oh Sally – I'll be the first one in our family to get divorced – do you know that Sis? The first one! God – the shame of it all!

SALLY. So what? Stop beating yourself up about it will you! Nobody's a saint! Christ Almighty, even Nelson Mandela got a bloody divorce.

(Sound of a doorbell ringing.)

JILL. I'll have to go. There's someone at the door.

*(Spots fade out on **SALLY**. Lights fade up on Jill's home. **CAROL** enters. She is carrying a big bouquet of flowers, a box of chocolates and a bottle of wine for **JILL**.)*

CAROL. These are for you Jill.

*(She kisses **JILL** and hands over the gifts.)*

JILL. *(Surprised.)* Thank you.

CAROL. I know it's been a tough day for you.

JILL. Aaah thanks Carol, but you didn't have to bring me all this.

CAROL. *(Talking over **JILL**.)* Seeing the solicitor for the first time and all that.

JILL. Thanks for the recommendation. She was very nice with me...

CAROL. *(Interrupting.)* I've been there. Got the T-Shirt. And believe me it's an eye opener.

JILL. What is?

CAROL. Divorce. You never really know a man till you've divorced him!

JILL. I suppose you're right.

CAROL. *(Talking over* **JILL**.*)* Ten years it's been.

JILL. Sorry?

CAROL. Ten years since my divorce was finalised. Still – I suppose it's better to have loved and divorced than be stuck with the little twat forever.

> (**CAROL** *looks upset.*)

JILL. Oh Carol! Does it still hurt that much after all this time?

CAROL. Oh, I'm not upset about the divorce now... I'm just upset that I'm not a widow!

JILL. Carol!

CAROL. I am. At least then I'd have happy memories of our marriage.

JILL. I know what you mean.

CAROL. Not to mention the life insurance if he'd popped his clogs.

JILL. Carol!

CAROL. And the cottage – our little home. I loved that cottage!

> (**CAROL** *starts to cry a little, grabs a hanky from her handbag.*)

JILL. Don't let him upset you after all this time Carol. He's not worth it, he isn't.

> (**CAROL***s sobs subside.* **JILL** *consoles her.*)

CAROL. Oh Jill. I'm so so sorry that all of this has happened to you.

JILL. Hey...hey...come on now.

CAROL. It's hard to let go isn't it? I bet you still love him don't you?

JILL. Yes... No... Sometimes... Oh... I don't know! I hate the fact that he's treated me like shit and I still care about him...but do I still love him? Can you still love a cheater Carol? People don't cheat by chance...they cheat by choice!

CAROL. It's awful – just awful that that woman has stolen Andy from you.

JILL. Oh, I wouldn't call her a woman. Real women have more class than that.

CAROL. What do you mean?

JILL. Would a real woman steal another woman's husband? Would she? She's more like a snake in the grass if you ask me.

>   (**CAROL** *wails loudly, even more distraught.*)

Carol love, I know you mean well but...

CAROL. *(Wailing over* **JILL.***)* I'M A SNAKE! I'M A SNAKE ...

>   (**CAROL** *continues to cry.* **JILL** *is shocked.*)

JILL. What?

CAROL. I'm a snake!

JILL. You're a...? Oh...you're not! Please tell me you're not!

>   (**CAROL** *nods her head and wails.*)

CAROL. I'm going out with a married man!

JILL. Carol!

CAROL. I know... I know...

JILL. Who? Do I know him?

CAROL. Phil Ryland.

JILL. Phil Ryland?

CAROL. He used to sit by us in chemistry in school.

JILL. Phil Ry...? That little short arse!

CAROL. He's a lot taller now.

JILL. I bet he is! How? How did you...?

CAROL. He got in touch with me on Facebook...after that school reunion...you didn't go to remember?

JILL. School reunion...that was five years ago! You've been seeing him for five years?

(CAROL nods.)

Who's he married to? Do you know her?

CAROL. No...and I don't want to either.

(Pause. JILL is shocked by the disclosure.)

JILL. Try and think about his wife will you.

CAROL. The least I know about her the better.

JILL. Why Carol? Why him?

(Pause as CAROL pulls herself together.)

CAROL. He makes me laugh...and I really love him!

JILL. But five years Carol! How can you let it go on that long?

CAROL. Because he adores his wife...he'll never leave her. I know that. He's made that clear from the start. And she knows what he's like – she knows he has other women. As long as he doesn't rub her nose in it she's fine about it all.

JILL. So he says.

CAROL. Yes.

JILL. And you believe him?

(CAROL nods again.)

CAROL. Yes.

> (**JILL** *is exasperated.*)

Oh forgive me Jill – please!

JILL. Me – forgive you?

CAROL. I've felt so guilty about it all, especially since Andy left you.

JILL. Don't! Don't bring me into this Carol.

CAROL. ...so guilty about seeing a married man...

> (*Pause.*)

Can we still be friends?

> (**JILL** *eventually answers.*)

JILL. Still friends? ... I suppose so...

> (**CAROL** *gets up to leave. She is visibly upset.*)

CAROL. The trouble is...at our age...most of the good ones have already been taken.

> (**CAROL** *runs offstage.* **JILL** *watches her go and turns to talk to the audience.*)

JILL. There are so many different ways to cheat aren't there? She's cheating herself because she thinks he's being honest with her, and he's cheating on her with his wife! The lying short arsed little bastard! ... Talking of lying bastards...

> (**JILL** *exits as classic rock song plays.*[*] *The music continues as the next scene is set centre stage – a small bistro/cafe. A flamboyant*

---

[*] A licence to produce *Head Over Heels* does not include a performance licence for any third-party or copyrighted recordings. Licensees should create their own.

> **WAITER** *carries on a bistro table and two chairs. He lays a checked tablecloth and menu on the table, and takes his position to greet customers.* **ANDY** *enters and the* **WAITER** *shows him to his seat.* **ANDY** *checks the menu and orders some coffee. The music plays throughout this sequence, eventually fading as* **JILL** *enters.* **ANDY** *waves her over.)*

ANDY. Hi.

JILL. Hi.

ANDY. I've just ordered some coffee.

> *(He waves the* **WAITER** *back over.* **JILL** *examines the menu.)*

WAITER. Yes?

ANDY. If we could just order some coffee for the lady...

JILL. Americano for me please.

WAITER. Certainly Madam. Are you both eating today?

> *(**ANDY** and **JILL** both answer at the same time.)*

ANDY. Yes.

JILL. No.

> *(**ANDY** looks surprised.)*

ANDY. Are you sure? I thought we could have a quick bite while we...

JILL. *(Interrupting.)* I'm sure. No thanks.

WAITER. Are you eating Sir?

ANDY. Er...no. On second thoughts I'll just have coffee.

WAITER. Yours was an Americano too wasn't it?

ANDY. Yes.

WAITER. Be with you both in a second.

(*The* **WAITER** *exits with a flourish.*)

(*Awkward pause.*)

ANDY. You're looking well.

(*Pause.*)

How's Danny?

JILL. OK.

(*Pause.*)

ANDY. I'm meeting up with him for a drink next week.

JILL. Are you?

ANDY. He rang me…finally!

JILL. Oh?

ANDY. He hadn't responded to any of my messages…until yesterday.

JILL. Really?

ANDY. Suppose it's understandable…in the circumstances.

JILL. Hmmmm.

ANDY. I mean…he's bound to take your side isn't he?

(**JILL** *toys with the menu.*)

But he is our son remember – not just yours. I hope that you haven't been filling his head with all sorts of nonsense about me.

(**JILL** *doesn't respond, and glances over to see if the coffee is on the way.*)

Well, have you?

(**JILL** *stares at him.*)

Have you?

JILL. I'm not responding to those ridiculous comments about Danny. The truth of the matter is that it's your birthday next week – and I reminded him about it – so that's why he got in touch with you.

> *(The argument is interrupted by the **WAITER** arriving at their table with the coffee. He places them on the table with a flourish.)*

WAITER. There you go. Two Americanos.

ANDY. Thanks.

WAITER. Enjoy!!!

> *(The **WAITER** exits. **JILL** spends a long time stirring in some sugar. **ANDY** sips his coffee. Eventually **JILL** breaks the silence.)*

JILL. We need to talk about money…finances…and agree on a mediator.

ANDY. Yes.

> *(**JILL** takes some paperwork out of her handbag and hands it to **ANDY**.)*

JILL. This is a summary of how I think we should split our income while the divorce proceedings are underway. I suggest you read it at your leisure and get back to me as soon as possible.

ANDY. You're organised!

JILL. So are you.

ANDY. What do you mean?

JILL. The first week you left you set up a new bank account.

ANDY. *(Spluttering.)* Well…we're not together now are we? And if I'm living with Tina the least I can do is pay my way.

JILL. Lucky old Tina. Finally she's a kept woman.

(**ANDY** *starts looking at the financial list* **JILL** *has given him.*)

ANDY. I don't know if I can afford this much Jill.

JILL. Oh yes you can.

ANDY. I don't have to pay for your...

JILL. *(Interrupting.)* I've done a little digging since you left. And over the last year you've been stashing money away like there's no tomorrow.

ANDY. I have no idea what...

JILL. *(Talking over him.)* Don't deny it...and you'd better be honest when we finally split our assets – or I am going to screw you for every penny that you've got!

(**ANDY** *looks sheepish.*)

(Pause.)

Have you seen a solicitor yet?

ANDY. Have you?

JILL. Yes. Miss Hyde of Ditchem Quick and Hyde. Yours?

ANDY. Mr Forth...of Bicker Back and Forth.

JILL. I'll tell my solicitor to get in touch with yours. You'll find contact details at the foot of the page. Plus the details of a mediator – Mr Allhart.

ANDY. Fine. I'll pass the information on.

(Pause as they both drink their coffee.)

I'm assuming that *you'll* file for divorce?

JILL. Sorry?

ANDY. I haven't really got any grounds have I? So you should…on the grounds of…

JILL. *(Loudly finishing the sentence for him.)* ADULTERY?

(**ANDY** *hushes her.*)

ANDY. Yes… *(Quietly.)* adultery.

JILL. I don't know if I want to do that.

ANDY. No?

JILL. *(Sincerely.)* We could just live apart for two years and then have the marriage dissolved. It'll give us more time to think things through…and our Danny won't have to watch us write horrible things about each other in divorce papers.

ANDY. NO! No… I can't do that. We'd… I mean I'd…rather it was a quick divorce.

JILL. Why? I'm not going to press for reconciliation.

ANDY. You wouldn't?

JILL. No… I wouldn't dream of it. If another woman steals your man, there's no better revenge than letting her keep the bastard is there?

(Pause.)

ANDY. I'll have to think about that – and I'm not promising anything! But you need to think about the house.

JILL. The house?

ANDY. I'll give you till Christmas. I think that's only fair. Then it'll be four months since I …er…left…and then you'll have to put it on the market.

JILL. On the market?

ANDY. It does belong to both of us remember. 50/50 and all that.

JILL. 50/50 split of all joint assets – in a way that suits both parties. And that doesn't suit me. Besides – you've got a home – all shacked up with Old Spice – slippers by her fire all nice and cozy. You'd have never run off with a bag lady that's for sure.

ANDY. Her money has got nothing to do with our divorce.

JILL. What would happen to me and Danny if the house was sold? That's our home.

ANDY. He's twenty-five! He's not a little lad anymore. He can always rent a flat in town.

JILL. And me?

ANDY. You? Well…we all have to move on…get on with the rest of our lives. And you'll meet someone else, I'm sure you will…eventually.

*(**JILL** is disgusted with him.)*

JILL. Just like that eh? Well, I suppose I might not be the woman that you want now, but at least I'm not the one that everyone else has had.

ANDY. Stop that now Jill.

JILL. Why? So you don't have to hear me say that you're the biggest disappointment of my entire life? Do you know – I loved being married to you Andy – I really did. It was great to find that one person who I thought would have my back for the rest of my life. And I honestly thought I'd found Mr Right. I just didn't know his first name was Always…

ANDY. If you're going to carry on like that I…

JILL. *(Interrupting.)* The real difference between me and you is that in years to come you'll never even remember the date of our wedding anniversary…but I'll never forget it.

(**ANDY** *gets up and chucks a tenner on the table for the coffee.*)

ANDY. I think we're just about done for the day aren't we? See you at the mediators.

(**JILL** *ignores him.*)

(**ANDY** *exits.*)

(*She toys with her wedding ring. It is tight on her finger.*)

JILL'S VOICEOVER. For richer for poorer.

(*A '70s pop soul song starts to softly play.* The* **WAITER** *enters and approaches the table as* **JILL** *continues to struggle with taking her wedding ring off. He clears the cups onto his tray.* **JILL** *finally yanks off the ring, stands to leave and plonks the ring on the tray. He looks surprised.*)

JILL. Keep the change.

(*She walks off – he stares at the ring and shouts after her.*)

WAITER. Thanks!

(*A '70s pop song* fades up as the waiter clears the set of the bistro table and two chairs. As he clears the last piece of the bistro set* **SALLY** *and* **JUDY** *enter wearing Christmas accessories eg silly hats/earrings etc.* **SALLY** *carries the pub's Christmas menu. They both have a glass of wine and a bottle and an empty glass for* **JILL** *who will join them later.*)

---

* A licence to produce *Head Over Heels* does not include a performance licence for any third-party or copyrighted recordings. Licensees should create their own.

(**JUDY** *carries a big sprig of mistletoe and gives the waiter a jolly kiss on the cheek as he finally exits. The music fades out.* **JUDY** *and* **SALLY** *sit in the pub.*)

(*Sound effects of a noisy bar.*)

(**JILL** *and* **DANNY** *enter.* **SALLY** *waves them over.*)

SALLY. Yoo hoo. Over here!

(**JILL** *and* **DANNY** *join the others at the table.* **JUDY** *pours* **JILL** *a drink.* **DANNY** *gives his Aunty* **SALLY** *a quick peck on the cheek before he sits.* **DANNY** *is wearing a Christmas sweater.*)

JUDY. There you go Jill. Do you want a glass Danny?

DANNY. No thanks Judy. I'm just dropping mum off.

SALLY. Off to another Christmas do are you?

DANNY. (*Indicating his sweater.*) How did you guess Aunty Sally?

SALLY. Hey. Less of the 'Aunty' in public! It makes me feel ancient now you're so grown up!

JUDY. I used to love going to the office parties at Christmas. I quite miss all that now I'm retired.

SALLY. You're not missing much believe me.

JUDY. No?

SALLY. Let's face it – most office Christmas parties are full of people catching up with other people that they haven't seen for – oooh let me see now – at least twenty minutes!

JUDY. Ignore her Danny.

DANNY. Yeah – I will! Anyway Aunty Sally – sorry – I mean 'Sally' – it's a free bar tonight – so it should be a great night.

SALLY. Well just don't drink too much then.

DANNY. Hey – I'll have you know that my drinking is completely under control…it's just my drunken behaviour that I need to work on!

*(They all laugh except **JILL** who suddenly gets up.)*

JILL. I'm just off to the ladies. Won't be long.

(They watch her rush off.)

SALLY. How's she getting on Danny?

DANNY. Up and down you know. But more down than up at the moment.

JUDY. It's hard for her isn't it?

SALLY. First Christmas without your Dad at home. Hard for both of you.

DANNY. More difficult for her than me I think.

SALLY. Well you're both at mine for Christmas day – two o' clock – don't forget!

DANNY. I won't. And I'm bringing some board games with me.

SALLY. Don't bring the bloody Monopoly again! It always ends in a row coz somebody cheats the banker.

DANNY. That's half the fun!

JUDY. What about your Dad? Are you seeing him over Christmas?

DANNY. Yep. Boxing Day tea time.

SALLY. With her?

DANNY. Mum? Noooo.

SALLY. I meant Tina.

DANNY. She'll probably be there. I think that he's on a tight leash now...

JUDY. It must be hard to be nice to that woman, after what she's done to your mum.

DANNY. Being nice to someone you don't respect isn't that hard Judy – and I'm just trying to behave like an adult...which is more than my Dad's done lately.

(**JILL** *re-enters and joins the table.*)

JILL. Are you off now love? You don't want to be late.

DANNY. Right! Better go. Are you getting a taxi home mum? Are you sure that you don't want me to swing by later and we can go home together?

JILL. No...no. Don't be daft. Off you trot and have a good time.

(**DANNY** *says his goodbyes.* **JILL** *watches him go. She smiles weakly at* **SALLY** *and* **JUDY**, *and refills her glass.*)

Cheers.

SALLY & JUDY. Cheers.

SALLY. Danny's looking well.

JILL. Yes...

(**JILL** *looks upset.*)

JUDY. What is it Jill?

SALLY. Oh God no – Andy hasn't finally made you put the house on the market has he?

(**JILL** *shakes her head.*)

JILL. No...no...not yet anyway... It's Danny.

SALLY. What's the matter with him?

JILL. Nothing's the matter. Actually it's good news.

> *(**JILL** is struggling not to cry but manages to hold herself together.)*

> *(**SALLY** and **JUDY** wait for her to finish her sentence.)*

He's moving to Birmingham…in a month's time.

SALLY. Birmingham?

JILL. With his job. He's been promoted.

JUDY. Oh – that's good news Jill!

> *(**JILL** is still struggling not to cry.)*

JILL. Yes…yes…it is. And I'm really happy for him… I mean…he's twenty-five now so it's about time he… moved on…and…

> *(She finally cries and **SALLY** gives her a hanky. **JILL** noisily blows her nose and wails.)*

I am s…s…sooooo p…p…pleased for him. I really am!

> *(She cries loudly. **SALLY** pats her back.)*

> *(Noddy Holder's voice suddenly bellows out the start of a Christmas song* as **JILL** cries. **SALLY** and **JUDY** exchange looks. **JILL** starts to calm down a little bit. She smiles apologetically.)*

Sorry about that girls,

SALLY. When did he tell you?

---

* A licence to produce *Head Over Heels* does not include a performance licence for any third-party or copyrighted recordings. Licensees should create their own.

JILL. This morning... I think he's been putting it off... breaking the news...because I'll be on my own when he goes. I didn't want to cry in front of him.

JUDY. I know how you feel. It's hard when they finally fly the nest for good.

JILL. I told him... I said... "I'm really really happy for you *(She blows her nose again.)* but when you move... to make you feel at home... I'm breaking into your house to eat all your food... I'm making a mess in your bathroom...and I'm throwing all my dirty washing on your bedroom floor..."

(They all manage to giggle through her tears.)

SALLY. Look on the bright side. You'll have the whole house to yourself.

JUDY. You can be totally selfish for the first time in your life.

SALLY. A brand new start.

JUDY. AND ...you can do whatever you want, whenever you want <u>with anyone you want</u>!

SALLY. Yeah!

*(**JILL** does not look convinced.)*

JUDY. Sooooo...is there anyone you fancy doing whatever whenever with?

JILL. Judy!

SALLY. Have you thought about internet dating?

JUDY. They're all looking for love online nowadays.

JILL. No thanks girls. Whoever said 'Love is all you need' is a bloody liar.

SALLY. What about a good holiday then when Danny's moved? Go on a little cruise somewhere.

JILL. I haven't got the money for a holiday. I'm still paying legal bills.

JUDY. Pay for it on your credit card – go on – fly abroad and catch some winter sun.

(The pub scene 'freezes'. A '60s folk song plays. **JILL** is in a spotlight and watches as a loved up **ANDY** and **TINA** walk into another spot dressed for their holiday in the sun. **ANDY** struggles with all the suitcases as **TINA** surveys the plane. They mime the scene, using their suitcases as seats. The **PILOT** enters swigging whisky out of a hip flask – he is blind drunk. He takes his position and holds the controls. They all mime the steep take off and the plane banking from side to side. Then the sound of the engine failing badly, and the plane nose diving. **TINA** and **ANDY** scream as the pilot struggles to control the plane. Pandemonium. Spectacular crash. Spot on them snaps off. **JILL** smiles in her spotlight and speaks to the audience.)*

JILL. Fantasy one hundred and four!

(Lights up again on the pub scene.)

SALLY. Get abroad for some sun... Andy's jetted off on loads of holidays with her!

JILL. I know. Never mind. I may be pale now but she'll be wrinkly later. Where's Carol?

SALLY. She can't make it today. Something came up at the last minute.

---

* A licence to produce *Head Over Heels* does not include a performance licence for any third-party or copyrighted recordings. Licensees should create their own.

JUDY. An old schoolfriend – Phillipa? She's meeting up with her.

SALLY. You must know her Jill.

JUDY. Carol said that she was in your year at school.

JILL. Phillipa? Oh yes… Phillipa! Short girl. She sat by us in Chemistry.

JUDY. Are we eating now? I'm absolutely starving.

SALLY. I'm having the full biftas. I know I'm gonna look like a Christmas pudding by January but I just don't care.

JILL. I'm not that hungry. I might have a salad.

SALLY. Don't start all that. No great new sex life starts with a salad!

JUDY. How about lamb shank? You love that.

JILL. Sounds good – I'll go for the lamb then.

JUDY. I'll go the bar and order. Two Christmas Dinners – and one lamb shank? We'll order pudding after – see how we go on.

(**JUDY** *exits.*)

SALLY. How are the divorce proceedings going? Or does it all grind to a halt over Christmas?

JILL. He's off on holiday – again – so that slows things down a bit.

SALLY. I hope you're going to put up a fight about the house.

JILL. I feel too tired to fight.

SALLY. Still not sleeping?

JILL. Not that well – but it's getting better.

SALLY. Well – get your solicitor to fight for you! You're paying her enough.

JILL. Yeah – don't think I've very been so stony broke.

SALLY. Get on her case then.

JILL. I can't blame her for all the delays – and she's a tough one alright. I think she was a cage fighter in a past life. Anyway – let's not talk about all that today eh? I just need to chill out.

> (**JUDY** *re-enters. She carries a bottle of Prosecco.*)

JUDY. The foods all ordered. More booze anyone?

> (**JUDY** *pours the drinks as they chat.*)

SALLY. Let's get this party started!

JUDY. Hey – I heard a cracking Christmas joke yesterday!

SALLY. Go on then – tell us.

JUDY. Why is a Christmas tree better than a man?

JILL & SALLY. I don't know. Why is a Christmas tree better than a man?

JUDY. Because it stays up for twelve days, has cute balls, and looks good with the lights on!

> (*They all laugh and raise their glasses.*)

ALL. Merry Christmas!

> (*A '70s pop song plays.* [*] *The lights quickly fade on the pub scene.*)

---

[*] A licence to produce *Head Over Heels* does not include a performance licence for any third-party or copyrighted recordings. Licensees should create their own.

(**SALLY** and **JUDY** *exit as a postman enters. He and* **JILL** *meet in a central spotlight and he hands her a letter before he exits singing along to the tune.*)

(**JILL** *opens the letter and reads it, growing increasingly angry as she does so.*)

(*Lights come up on her solicitor's office where* **MS HYDE** *is sat.* **JILL** *joins her as the music and central spotlight fade out.*)

(*She stands over* **MS HYDE** *brandishing the letter.*)

JILL. I can't believe it!

MS HYDE. I can't say that I'm surprised.

JILL. He hasn't got any grounds!

MS HYDE. That doesn't seem to bother him.

JILL. All these things he's written about me!

MS HYDE. I know.

JILL. (*Reading from the court letter.*) According to this we never had sex, I spent every penny he had, and I was the most unreasonable person walking the earth to live with. It's just not true!

MS HYDE. He obviously doesn't want to wait for two years, and she didn't want to be named on divorce papers if you'd filed first on the grounds of adultery.

JILL. I'm going to fight it!

MS HYDE. Are you?

JILL. I'm not giving him the satisfaction! It's such a load of lies! He screws her, leaves me, treats me like shit – and then files for divorce against me? What is going on?

MS HYDE. I understand your frustrations Jill – but by wanting to wait two years you've given Titillating Tina and your husband a lot of time to discuss things.

JILL. It's just so…cruel! Oh God – sometimes I wish I could order Karma online – I really do.

MS HYDE. The reality is that she'll have convinced him by now that he had every right to leave you for her, he'll have convinced himself that she's right, and they'll both have convinced themselves that the divorce is all your fault.

JILL. I want to appeal against it. I'm not having that read out in court about me.

MS HYDE. Disputing it would end up costing you a LOT more in legal costs, and I know you're struggling financially at the moment.

(Pause.)

Look – these things are read in small impersonal rooms by a Judge and a clerk – not read out in a huge court of law for everyone to hear. In truth it's just a bit of paper that will end your marriage. The really important thing you need to ask yourself is will any of your friends and family believe a word he has said?

JILL. No – not one.

MS HYDE. And at the end of the day that's what really counts isn't it?

(Pause.)

He's also written a list of personal items that he wants to collect from the house. He's legally entitled to access to the marital home so long as he gives you notice – so you need to sort this out as soon as possible.

*(**MS HYDE** hands **JILL** the list.)*

My advice is – let him make a fool of himself more than he already has. Let him! Let him walk away with his little bit of paper and his little hypocritical victory. I'll include a legal line before you sign anything stating that his allegations are TOTALLY overinflated – but I wouldn't bother fighting it if I were you.

JILL. You wouldn't?

MS HYDE. No! Why waste your money fighting it when everyone who knows you will think so much less of him for doing this to you? Choose your battles carefully Jill – and spend your money wisely – by fighting for what really matters to you now.

Your home.

> *(**MS HYDE** pulls a camouflage flak jacket out of one of the desk cupboards and slams it on the desk.)*

Your share of the assets.

> *(She slams a military helmet on the desk and a bullet belt plus grenades.)*

And your future.

> *(She slams a huge machine gun on the desk.)*
>
> *(**MS HYDE** puts on a Homburg Hat and puffs on a huge cigar – she is now Churchill.)*

THIS *(She does the Churchillian victory sign.)* IS WAR!

> *(Air raid sirens suddenly blare out and anti aircraft lights fill the stage.)*
>
> *(**MS HYDE** helps **JILL** on with her war apparel and then leaves the set. **JILL** pans the set with her machine gun.)*
>
> *(**ANDY** enters dressed as Rambo and carrying a For Sale sign.)*

(The mediator marches on dressed as a UN peace keeper and carrying a huge blue banner/flag. He takes up a commanding position centre stage as the sirens begin to fade out, and a '70s soul song suddenly blasts out.*)

(The mediator mimes to the song as **ANDY** *and* **JILL** *embark on their conflict over the house in which* **ANDY** *tries to put the For Sale sign up and* **JILL** *does everything in her power to stop him. It should be a comical choreographed sequence, with the mediator intervening regularly if things look too violent.)*

(The sequence ends with **JILL** *managing to get hold of the For Sale sign, and then beating* **ANDY** *to the ground with it. The mediator intervenes [still singing along.] and helps the injured* **ANDY** *to his feet and offstage.)*

*(***JILL** *chucks the For Sale sign offstage after* **ANDY***, and poses triumphantly before she takes off the war gear as the music fades out.)*

(The scene changes to what is now legally **JILL***'s home.)*

(She kisses the wall and walks slowly round the room, overwhelmed by her victory.)

(The doorbell rings. **SALLY** *enters and indicates the house.)*

SALLY. Well?

---

* A licence to produce *Head Over Heels* does not include a performance licence for any third-party or copyrighted recordings. Licensees should create their own.

JILL. Mine...all mine!

> *(They dance hysterically round the room together and laugh.)*

SALLY. I am so chuffed for you Sis. So chuffed!

JILL. I can't believe it!

SALLY. So is it all done and dusted now – all sorted?

JILL. We've got to split some other stuff but... God! This is such a relief!

SALLY. Does Danny know yet?

JILL. I'll ring him tonight.

SALLY. How's his new job panning out?

JILL. Good.

SALLY. And Birmingham?

JILL. He's a *Peaky Blinders* fan so he loves it!

> *(They both laugh.)*

Are you stopping for a cup of coffee?

SALLY. No thanks. I've just shot round in my lunch hour. We're not all retired yet you know! Anyway – to celebrate I've brought you these.

> *(She hands **JILL** a bunch of flowers and a parcel.)*

JILL. Thanks!

SALLY. Open it then...

JILL. You're spoiling me! I hope it's not chocolates coz I'll eat the whole box to celebrate.

> *(She opens the box and holds up the present. It is a vibrator.)*

Is this what I think it is?

SALLY. The latest deluxe version. Spoil yourself! Not right now of course.

JILL. You can spoil yourself without one of these you know Sally.

SALLY. Oh yes?

JILL. I've got news for you. If God didn't want us to masturbate he's have made our arms a lot shorter.

SALLY. Jill! *(She laughs.)* You've got needs! And I still think you should try internet dating.

JILL. I'll let you know when I do.

SALLY. *(Checks her watch.)* Oh shit – I'm gonna be late for work. Gotta go!

(She jumps up.)

Happy days eh?

JILL. Yeah. Happy days.

(They hug each other.)

SALLY. Bye big sis.

JILL. Bye little sis.

*(**SALLY** exits. **JILL** turns to the audience. She is still holding the vibrator.)*

Looks a bit scary.

(She turns it on. It vibrates. She listens to it.)

Bit noisy too...

(She immediately looks bored and turns it off.)

It's no good. I'm not in the mood.

*(She busies herself looking at the flowers **SALLY** had bought her.)*

Lovely! Flowery and pretty. I'm in this sort of mood today! ... You know, I still can't get over those divorce papers – Andy making out I never wanted sex! I did want sex – but I wanted good sex – not him falling asleep once he'd got what he wanted, or answering his bloody mobile if it rang in the middle of it all! Plus I didn't always have time to rip off my Bridget Jones knickers and pop on some sexy lingerie before he hit the bedroom... mind you – he always loved a bit of role playing...

*(Spot snaps on **JILL** as an American detective TV theme tune blasts out.*)*

(Lights up central stage.)

*(**ANDY** rushes on in a smart suit and carrying a gun. He is the sharp shooting Captain Steve McGarrett [as played by Jack Lord in the TV series]. He checks out the set for bad guys and commands the stage.)*

*(**TINA** dances on in a hula skirt, a flowery hair piece, an alluring swimming costume. She is barefoot, and dances suggestively round him swivelling her hips.)*

(He stands immobile and strong. She puts her arms round his neck. They kiss.)

(He pulls back from her – initially looking enamoured with it all – but suddenly clutches at his heart. He is having a heart attack.)

---

* A licence to produce *Head Over Heels* does not include a performance licence for any third-party or copyrighted recordings. Licensees should create their own.

*(**TINA** panics, screams and holds him up. He clutches at her as they struggle offstage and his dark wig comes off in his hand.)*

JILL'S VOICEOVER. In sickness and in health – till death do us part!

*(**JILL** smiles at the audience.)*

JILL. I've lost count now, have you? Only joking! One hundred and five!

(Her mobile rings.)

Hello? Oh…it's you Andy… Yes…yes… I've got your list. No…no… I haven't had time to sort it all out yet. You'll have to give me a bit of time… Next Friday? Yes… I think I can get it altogether for then… Sorry? … OK then – see you at ten o'clock next Friday… Bye.

(She hangs up and stares for a long time at the phone. She retrieves Andy's list from her handbag and scans it.)

*(As she exits a cheesy 70's **GAME SHOW HOST** enters to thunderous canned applause. He takes centre stage in showbizzy lighting, and mimes to the theme tune of a popular gameshow*, striking an iconic pose as the song ends. Thunderous canned applause.)*

*(Totally unaware of him, **JILL** criss crosses the stage as she gathers items for **ANDY**. The impression should be that she is moving things on **ANDY**'s list from the one side of the stage to the offstage garage for him to collect.)*

---

* A licence to produce *Head Over Heels* does not include a performance licence for any third-party or copyrighted recordings. Licensees should create their own.

(The conveyor belt music plays as this sequence of events is acted out. The **GAME SHOW HOST** carries a microphone, and the music underscores his commentary as he comments on the things **JILL** is taking to the garage.)*

GAME SHOW HOST. Hello ladies and gentlemen. Nice to see you, to see you… *(Waits for the audience to join in.)* Nice!

And on the divorce conveyor belt tonight we have!!!!!!!!!!

An antique carriage clock, *(Aside.)* Andy's obviously got problems letting go of his past.

An electric drill *(Aside.)* a little tool for him to use going round and round in circles till he dies of old age.

A leaf blower, *(Aside.)* well – windbags do like to stick together don't they?

An espresso machine, *(Aside.)* How is divorce like an espresso? *(He gets the audience to say "I don't know – how is a divorce like an espresso".)* It's expensive and bitter!

Egg coddlers, *(Aside.)* Egg coddlers?? Whatever the hell they are…

Various expensive malt whiskies, *(Aside.)* You know what they say about that don't you? Whisky is risky – but it makes the girls go frisky! Watch out Tina!

A collection of superhero comic books, *(Aside.)* for the man who acts like the superhero – or villain – in your life.

---

* A licence to produce *Head Over Heels* does not include a performance licence for any third-party or copyrighted recordings. Licensees should create their own.

Original paintings and a bronze sculpture, *(Aside.)* I think Andy's a bit of an artist – no – I do – really I do – living in a fantasy world with unrealistic expectations.

And not forgetting – a cuddly toy! Hurray !! *(He gets the audience to cheer and then says his aside.)* Always my favourite!

Finally – last but not least – half of a classic vinyl collection of seventies pop music.

> *(**JILL** does not appear with the vinyl He looks for her and loudly repeats.)*

AND FINALLY ... A CLASSIC VINYL COLLECTION OF SEVENTIES POP MUSIC!

> *(She still does not appear.)*

> *(He shrugs his shoulders, looks bemused, then addresses the audience.)*

Didn't she do well!!!!!

> *(He takes a corny bow and exits to the game show theme music* and thunderous canned applause.)*

> *(The central spot fades and full set lights come up.)*

> *(**ANDY** enters unseen by her. He looks around the house for what may well be his last time. **JILL** enters.)*

> *(She looks surprised that **ANDY** is in the house. He holds up his front door key.)*

---

* A licence to produce *Head Over Heels* does not include a performance licence for any third-party or copyrighted recordings. Licensees should create their own.

ANDY. I'm surprised that you haven't changed the locks.

> (**ANDY** *goes to put the keys back in his pocket but* **JILL** *holds her hand out, and he gives her the key.*)

JILL. I haven't quite finished getting all the stuff together

ANDY. *(Talking over her.)* It's OK. I'm a bit early. Just a bit anxious to get it all done and dusted coz we're away to the...the er... *(Realises he is digging a hole for himself.)* ...to the...erm...airport at twelve.

JILL. Anywhere nice?

ANDY. Tenerife.

JILL. *(Sarcastically.)* Lovely.

> (*Pause.*)

ANDY. Sooooo. Is it all ready then?

JILL. I've already put the stuff you want in the garage. I've left it by the door – and it's not locked. Just close it when you've finished.

ANDY. Fine.

> (*He starts checking his copy of the list that he has in his hand...* **JILL** *watches him.*)

JILL. It's all there.

ANDY. Records – the vinyl – is that all there?

JILL. Oh yeah – the vinyl. I haven't sorted that out yet.

ANDY. Well, it is 50/50, so I am entitled to...

JILL. *(Interrupting.)* I'm not arguing about it Andy.

ANDY. Meaning?

JILL. Meaning I just want things to be fair. And I bought all the vinyl so I'm keeping it. OK?

ANDY. Oh… OK then…right…alright then.

(Long pause.)

Look, I know it's been a big shock for you.

JILL. I'm not shocked anymore that you let me down Andy.

ANDY. I know things aren't the same for you…

JILL. *(Interrupting him.)* You're right – it's not the same – it's a lot better actually.

(He doesn't believe her. He smiles.)

ANDY. Still a sarcastic bitch?

JILL. Still a pompous bastard?

*(**ANDY** looks around the room. This was his home for a long long time.)*

ANDY. I'm SO pissed off with you about the house!

JILL. Oh yeah? Well I'm pissed off with you about a lot of things – so if you want a row you've come to the right place for one.

ANDY. NO …no! Not today Jill. We've done enough of that.

(Pause.)

You know, it would be good if we could still be friends. For Danny's sake.

JILL. I can't see that happening any time soon.

ANDY. No?

JILL. Nah. You were my cup of tea once but I drink champagne now.

*(**ANDY** manages a quiet chuckle.)*

ANDY. Sometimes I wonder how on earth I ever put up with you.

JILL. Yeah? Well I put up with you too – for thirty-two years – so we're even.

> *(He chuckles again. She still amuses him.)*

You might not love me any more Andy – but at least I can still make you laugh.

ANDY. You always could…and I loved you for a long time Jill. I really did…

> *(Long pause – are they going to reconcile??)*

JILL. Wow!!!! That was a close call! I thought for a moment there that you give a fuck about what's gonna happen to me.

ANDY. Trust you to…

JILL. *(Interrupting.)* But I could tell that you were lying coz your lips were moving.

> *(**ANDY** shakes his head and gives a wry smile.)*

Your time is up I think.

ANDY. I think so too.

> *(He leaves. She watches him go. Turns to the audience.)*

JILL. The vinyl!

> *(She quickly exits and returns with a large pile of vinyl LPs.)*

End of an era.

> *(She kneels and methodically looks at each record. As her memories flood back we hear*

excerpts of the 70's playlist of the play.* Suggested song list appears at the beginning of the script.)

(The music fades out. She reconnects with the audience.)

End of one era…and the beginning of a new one! What Andy doesn't know is that I've started an online vintage vinyl store. A record exchange. It's been scary sorting it all out. It's something just for me – after all these years of looking after everyone else – and I know I'm gonna love it – I just know I am… It's my time now – my time!

(She shouts up to the tech box.)

LIGHTS …

*(Disco lights come on. Underlying music plays for **JILL**'s finale song.**)*

GIRLS …

*(**CAROL, JUDY** and **SALLY** all dance on in a choreographed way as **JILL**'s backing group.)*

*(**JILL** strikes a spotlit pose and faces the audience.)*

(She sings.)

I BET YOU'RE WONDERING NOW WHAT WILL HAPPEN NEXT.
WILL ANDY MEET A GRISLY END AS TINA CLUTCHES AT HIS NECK?

---

* A licence to produce *Head Over Heels* does not include a performance licence for any third-party or copyrighted recordings. Licensees should create their own.
** A licence to produce *Head Over Heels* does not include a performance licence for any third-party or copyrighted recordings. Licensees should create their own.

SHOULD I END ALL MY WILD FANTASIES, STOP FESTERING ON THE PAST
ACCEPT MY MARRIAGE'S OVER AND THAT SOME THINGS JUST DON'T LAST?
CAN I LET GO OF ALL THOSE YEARS, ALL THOSE YEARS
OF LOVE AND LAUGHTER, CAN I OVERCOME MY FEARS?
FEARS OF BEING ON MY OWN, OF BECOMING A SAD SACK
FEARS OF BEING INDEPENDENT, FEARS THAT NO-ONE'S GOT MY BACK ...

(Dramatic pause...)

Well... I have THRIVED! Oh how I've thrived!

I've moved on – achieved so many things – and yes I've had to strive.

Strive to build a better future, strive to build my self-esteem.

Strive to continue on life's journey and to finally live my dream.

AND I'VE ARRIVED! ... Hey Hey...

(Music continues for a choreographed curtain call.*)

Blackout
End

---

* A licence to produce *Head Over Heels* does not include a performance licence for any third-party or copyrighted recordings. Licensees should create their own.

Milton Keynes UK
Ingram Content Group UK Ltd.
UKHW020452260924
448856UK00010B/274

9 780573 000683